ALBERT SCHWEITZER

A John Macrae Book

Henry Holt and Company   New York

Out of My Life and Thought

An Autobiography

Newly translated by Antje Bultmann Lemke
Preface by Rhena Schweitzer Miller
and Antje Bultmann Lemke

Henry Holt and Company, Inc.
Publishers since 1866
115 West 18th Street
New York, New York 10011

Henry Holt® is a registered trademark
of Henry Holt and Company, Inc.

Library of Congress Cataloging-in-Publication Data
Schweitzer, Albert, 1875–1965.
[Aus meinem Leben und Denken. English]
Out of my life and thought : an autobiography / Albert Schweitzer ;
translated by Antje Bultmann Lemke ; foreword by Rhena Schweitzer
Miller and Antje Bultmann Lemke.
p.   cm.
Translation of: Aus meinem Leben und Denken.
Includes index.
1. Schweitzer, Albert, 1875–1965.   2. Strasbourg (France)—Biography.
3. Missionaries, Medical—Gabon—Lambaréné (Moyen Ogooué)—Biography.
4. Theologians—Europe—Biography.   5. Musicians—Europe—Biography.
I. Title.
CT1018.S45A282   1990   90-37697
610'.92—dc20   CIP
[B]

ISBN 0-8050-1467-5
ISBN 0-8050-1862-X (An Owl Book: pbk.)

First hardcover revised edition published in 1990 by
Henry Holt and Company, Inc.

First Owl Book Edition—1991

Designed by Paula R. Szafranski

Printed in the United States of America
All first editions are printed on acid-free paper.∞

10   9   8   7   6   5   4   3   2   1
10   9   8   7   6   5   (pbk.)

Contents

vi **Contents**

Photographs follow page 146.

Preface

"I want to be the pioneer of a new Renaissance. I want to throw faith in a new humanity like a burning torch into our dark times." So Albert Schweitzer proclaimed in the preface to his book *Civilization and Ethics* in 1923.

Out of My Life and Thought, the book he considered his most important, provides the key to understanding the man, his thought, and his work. It is the testimony of this pioneer whose philosophy of respect for all life is essential if we are to succeed in moving from the dark ages of religious and political strife toward a new Renaissance embracing the recognition of human rights, of environmental responsibilities, and of political interdependence.

In this book he describes how he became Schweitzer the theologian, the philosopher, the musician, and the medical doctor. The many facets of his personality, his abundance of knowledge in such different fields made him the active and spiritual center of his hospital in Lambaréné and a figure of worldwide influence and recognition.

As to the origin of his autobiography, he told the readers of the first edition of 1931: "In 1925 I wrote a forty-two-page account for the seventh volume of the scholarly series *Contemporary Philosophy in Self-Portraits*, published by Felix Meiner in Leipzig. . . . When this treatise was published as a separate book, many readers took it to be an account of my whole life and thought. To remedy this misconception I decided to complete the initial study in such a way that it would tell not only about my scholarly work but also about my life and thought in general."

Out of My Life and Thought is the only book Schweitzer completed in Africa, and thirty years later he wrote to a friend in Paris: "That I was able to write this book I owe to the two physicians who assisted me in Lambaréné. When they heard about the publisher's interest, they offered to take over some of my work so I could be at the hospital only in the morning. By writing every afternoon and until midnight, I was able to complete the manuscript in five months. Later on I could never have taken so much time off to concentrate on my writing. It gave me the opportunity to express my thoughts on religion, on philosophy and the arts, and to pave the way for my reflections on the principle of Reverence for Life, which can

motivate us to return to a civilization that is determined
by humanism."

The first German edition of 1931 was translated by
Schweitzer's friend C. T. Campion and published in 1933
by Allen & Unwin in London and by Henry Holt in New
York. Other translations followed, and at last count there
were nineteen, from Chinese and Czech to Tamil and Tu-
legu. Some translations, for example that of 1959 in Oriyan,
an Indian language, include prefatory letters by Hermann
Hesse and Père Dominique Pire.

According to the notes in Schweitzer's personal German
copy, a French translation was intended as early as 1932.
Yet, as with several unfinished manuscripts, he did not find
the time to devote to this project.

In 1953 another attempt at a French edition was made,
when Madeleine France translated the German original.
Schweitzer wanted to review the manuscript before its
publication but he had other priorities. With his acceptance of the Nobel Peace Prize in 1954, his eightieth birthday in 1955, and his appeal in 1957 for a nuclear test ban,
his days and nights were filled with correspondence and
preparation of lectures, which were of pressing concern
to him.

Finally, in 1959, during his last sojourn in Europe,
Schweitzer spent three weeks in Paris. With his friend and
collaborator Robert Minder he edited the French translation, which was published in 1960 by Albin Michel in Paris.
When Schweitzer received the first copy in Lambaréné in
January 1960 he immediately wrote to the publisher, plead-
ing for removal of the wrapper that read: "Le grand docteur
vous parle." This statement, "The great doctor speaks to
you," reminded Schweitzer of Hitler's announcement "Le

Führer vous parle," to which the French had been exposed two decades earlier.

The French edition contains several changes from the German original, especially the deletion of passages Schweitzer considered either too technical—such as some of his reflections on theological subjects—or displeasing to the French reader. This edition has been most helpful in the preparation of the new English translation, since many convoluted German sentences and long paragraphs were rephrased and broken up. Some phrases have been replaced by precise, more assertive statements.

In addition to the French version, the new English translation is based on a copy of the German edition in the Archives Centrales Albert Schweitzer at Günsbach, which contains Schweitzer's own corrections, made between 1930 and 1960.

Cognizant of the fact that it is impossible to give an identical rendering of any literary text in a second language, this translation aims to be as faithful as possible to the author's own style. No attempt has been made to change Schweitzer's expressions, to "degenderize" or otherwise adjust the language in accordance with current trends. Special care has been taken with Schweitzer's explication of his philosophy and theology. Where the earlier version freely substituted *reason* for *spirit*, *scientific* for *scholarly*, *dogmatic* for *orthodox*, the original meaning of the German expression has been chosen. An *Evangelische Gemeinde* is a "Protestant parish" and not a group of Evangelical believers, and when Schweitzer speaks about *die Welt* he intends to include the whole world and not only mankind. Thus, the new translation hopes to clarify ambiguities and to come as close as possible to Schweitzer's language, his intentions, and his philosophy.

A chronology of the life of Albert Schweitzer, which follows the text, gives a quick overview of major events and completes the autobiography for the period until his death in 1965. For readers interested in other books by and about Schweitzer, a bibliography of selected titles in English has been included.

We want to express our deep gratitude to Gustav Woytt, a nephew of Schweitzer, who had worked for him for many years. He was familiar with the development and different translations of this book and graciously shared his knowledge. We owe to him and to the generous cooperation of the Archives Centrales Albert Schweitzer in Günsbach, France, that we have a broader knowledge of the genesis of this book.

Our warmest thanks go to Miss Elizabeth Gempp, who has encouraged and generously supported the preparation of this new edition. For the typing and editing we would like to express our gratitude to Eileen Snyder and Margaret Sevcenko.

Last but not least we would like to thank the members of Henry Holt and Company, especially Mr. John Macrae for the enthusiasm with which he received the manuscript, and his advice throughout the publishing process, and Amy Robbins for her perceptive suggestions and expert copy editing.

For the photographs we are indebted to the Archives Centrales Albert Schweitzer in Günsbach, France, the Albert Schweitzer Center in Great Barrington, Massachusetts, and the Albert Schweitzer Fellowship in New York.

As we move toward a new century it is amazing to see how the spirit of Albert Schweitzer has retained its freshness and authenticity. His life and thought, nurtured by German and French culture and by the philosophies of East and West, and forged by human service in Europe and Africa, can point the way toward a global society.

Rhena Schweitzer Miller
Antje Bultmann Lemke

DECEMBER 1989

Out of My Life
and Thought

Childhood, School, and University

1

I was born on January 14, 1875, at Kaysersberg in Upper Alsace, the second child of Louis Schweitzer, who at that time served as minister for the little flock of Protestants in that Catholic place. My paternal grandfather was schoolmaster and organist at Pfaffenhofen in Lower Alsace, and three of his brothers occupied similar posts. My mother, Adele, née Schillinger, was a daughter of the pastor of Mühlbach in the Münster Valley, Upper Alsace.

A few weeks after my birth my father moved to Günsbach in the Münster

Valley. Here with my three sisters and one brother I spent a happy childhood overshadowed only by my father's frequent illnesses. His health improved later on, however, and as a sturdy septuagenarian he looked after his parish during the war under the fire of the French guns that swept the valley from the heights of the Vosges mountains, destroying many a house and killing many an inhabitant of Günsbach. He died at a ripe old age in 1925. My mother had been run over and killed by cavalry horses on the road between Günsbach and Weier-im-Tal in 1916.

When I was five years old my father began giving me music lessons on the old square piano that we had inherited from grandfather Schillinger. He had no great technical skill but improvised charmingly. When I was seven I surprised our teacher by playing hymn tunes on the harmonium with harmonies I supplied myself. At eight, when my legs were hardly long enough to reach the pedals, I began to play the organ. My passion for that instrument was inherited from my grandfather Schillinger, who had been much interested in organs and organ building, and, as my mother told me, had a reputation for improvising magnificently. In every town he visited, he made a point of getting to know its organs. When the famous organ was installed in the Stiftskirche at Lucerne he journeyed there to see its builder at work.

I was nine years old when I was permitted for the first time to substitute for the organist at a service at Günsbach.

Till the autumn of 1884 I went to the Günsbach village school. After that, for a year I was at the Realschule (which is a secondary school giving no instruction in classical languages) at Münster, and there I had private lessons in Latin to prepare me for entering the fifth class in the Gymnasium.

In the autumn of 1885 I entered the Gymnasium at Mülhausen in Alsace. My godfather, Louis Schweitzer, my
grandfather's half brother, who was director of the primary
schools in that town, was kind enough to take me to live
with him. Otherwise my father, who had nothing beyond
his slender stipend on which to bring up his large family,
could hardly have afforded to send me to a Gymnasium.

The strict discipline to which I was subjected in the house
of my great-uncle and his wife, who had no children of their
own, was very good for me. It is with deep gratitude that
I always think of all the kindness I received from them.

Although it had cost me some trouble to learn to read
and write, I had got on fairly well in school at Günsbach
and Münster. At the Gymnasium, however, I was at first
a poor scholar. This was owing not solely to my being slack
and dreamy but partly also to the fact that my private lessons in Latin had not prepared me sufficiently for the fifth
class, in which I entered the school. It was only when my
teacher in the fourth, Dr. Wehmann, showed me how to
study properly and gave me some self-confidence that
things went better. But Dr. Wehmann's influence over me
was due above all to the fact, of which I became aware
during my first days in his class, that he prepared every
lesson he gave very carefully in advance. He became a
model of fulfillment of duty for me. I visited him many
times in later life. When, toward the end of the war, I went
to Strasbourg, where he lived during the latter part of his
life, I at once inquired after him. I learned, however, that
starvation had ruined his nervous system and that he had
taken his own life.

My music teacher at Mülhausen was Eugène Münch, the
young organist at the Reformed Church of St. Stephen.

This was his first post after leaving the Academy of Music at Berlin, where he had been seized by the then reawakening enthusiasm for Bach. I owe it to him that I became acquainted in my early years with the works of the cantor of St. Thomas and from my fifteenth year onward enjoyed the privilege of sound instruction on the organ. When, in the autumn of 1898, he died of typhoid fever in the flower of his age, I perpetuated his memory in a booklet written in French. It was published in Mülhausen, and was the first product of my pen to appear in print.

At the Gymnasium I was chiefly interested in history and natural science. In languages and mathematics it took a great deal of effort for me to accomplish anything. But after a time I felt a certain fascination in mastering subjects for which I had no special talent. Consequently, in the upper classes I was considered one of the better students, though not one of the best. With essays, however, if I remember rightly, I was usually the first.

In the first class we were taught Latin and Greek by the distinguished director of the Gymnasium, Wilhelm Deecke of Lübeck. His lessons were not the dry instruction of a mere linguist; they introduced us to ancient philosophy while giving us glimpses into contemporary thought. He was an enthusiastic follower of Schopenhauer.

On June 18, 1893, I passed my final examinations. In the written papers I did not do very well, not even in the essay. In the oral examination, however, I attracted the attention of the chairman of the board of examiners—Dr. Albrecht of Strasbourg—with my knowledge of history and my historical judgment. A "very good" in history, substantiated by some words of praise, adorned my diploma, which otherwise was quite mediocre.

In October of the same year, the generosity of my father's

elder brother, a businessman in Paris, secured for me the privilege of organ instruction from the Parisian organist Charles-Marie Widor. My teacher at Mülhausen had taught me so well that Widor, after hearing me play, took me as a pupil, although he normally confined his instruction to members of the organ class at the Conservatory. This instruction was for me an event of decisive importance. Widor presided over a fundamental improvement in my technique and made me strive to attain perfect plasticity in playing. At the same time, thanks to him, the meaning of the architectonic in music became clear to me.

My first lesson with Widor happened to be on the sunny October day when the Russian sailors under Admiral Avellan arrived in Paris for the visit that was the first manifestation of the Franco-Russian friendship then beginning. I was delayed by the closely packed, expectant crowds that filled the boulevards and the central streets, and was very late in reaching the master's house.

At the end of October 1893, I entered the University of Strasbourg. I lived in the theological seminary of St. Thomas (the Collegium Wilhelmitanum), the principal of which was the learned Reverend Alfred Erichson. Just at that time he was occupied with the completion of his great edition of the works of Calvin.

The University of Strasbourg, recently founded, already had a fine reputation. Unhampered by tradition, teachers and students alike strove to realize the ideal of a modern university. There were hardly any older professors among the faculty. A fresh breeze of youthfulness animated the whole university.

I took the two subjects of theology and philosophy together. As I had learned only the elements of Hebrew in the Gymnasium, my first term was spoiled by work for the "Hebraicum" (the preliminary examination in Hebrew), which I passed with much effort on February 17, 1894. Later, spurred on again by the effort to master what did not come easily to me, I acquired a sound knowledge of that language.

Anxiety about the Hebraicum did not prevent me from eagerly attending the lectures by Heinrich Julius Holtzmann on the Synoptics—that is to say, the three first Gospels—and others by Wilhelm Windelband and Theobald Ziegler on the history of philosophy.

On April 1, 1894, I began my year of military service, but the kindness of my captain, Krull by name, made it possible for me to be at the university by eleven o'clock almost every day, and so to attend Windelband's lectures.

When in the autumn of 1894 we went on maneuvers in the neighborhood of Hochfelden (Lower Alsace), I put my Greek Testament in my knapsack. I should explain that at the beginning of the winter term, those theological students who wished to compete for a scholarship had to pass an examination in three subjects. Those, however, who were then doing their military service had only to take one. I chose the synoptic Gospels.

I took my Greek New Testament with me to maneuvers so I would not disgrace myself with a poor performance before Holtzmann, whom I admired very much. At that time I was robust and did not know fatigue, so I could study in the evenings and on holidays. During the summer I had gone through Holtzmann's commentary. Now I wanted to get to know the text and see how much I remembered of his commentary and his lectures. This produced an amazing discovery. Holtzmann had gained recognition in scholarly circles for his hypothesis that the Gospel of Mark is the oldest, and that its plan serves as the basis for Matthew and Luke. That seemed to justify the conclusion that the public activities of Jesus can only be understood through Mark's Gospel. This conclusion puzzled me deeply. On one of the rest days, which we spent in the village of Guggenheim, I concentrated on the tenth and eleventh chapters of Matthew, and became aware of the significance of what is narrated in those two chapters by him alone, and not by Mark as well.

In the tenth chapter of Matthew the mission of the twelve disciples is narrated. As Jesus sends them out He tells them that they will almost immediately suffer severe persecution. But nothing of the kind happens.

He tells them also that the appearance of the Son of Man will take place before they have gone through the cities of Israel, which can only mean that the heavenly Messianic Kingdom is dawning. He has therefore no expectation of seeing them return.

How is it possible that Jesus leads His disciples to expect events that do not take place?

I was dissatisfied with Holtzmann's explanation that we are dealing not with a historical discourse about Jesus but with one made up at a later date, after His death, out of various "Sayings of Jesus." A later generation would never have gone so far as to put into His mouth words that were belied by the subsequent course of events.

The bare text compelled me to assume that Jesus was really announcing the persecution of the disciples, which would then be followed by the appearance of the supernatural Son of Man. This announcement, however, was proven wrong by subsequent events.

But how did He come to entertain such an expectation, and what must His feelings have been when events turned out otherwise than He had assumed they would?

Matthew 11 records the Baptist's question to Jesus, and the answer Jesus gave him. Here too it seemed to me that Holtzmann and the commentators in general do not sufficiently appreciate the riddles of the text. Whom does the Baptist mean when he asks Jesus whether He is "the one who is to come"? Is it then quite certain, I asked myself, that by the Coming One no one can be meant except the Messiah? According to late Jewish Messianic beliefs, the coming of the Messiah is to be preceded by that of his Forerunner, Elijah, risen from the dead, and to this previously expected Elijah Jesus applies the expression "the Coming One," when He tells the people around Him (Matthew 11:14) that the Baptist himself is Elijah who is to come. Therefore, I concluded, the Baptist in his question used the expression with that same meaning. He did not send his disciples to Jesus to ask Him whether He was the Messiah; he wanted to learn from Him, strange as it may seem to us, whether He was the expected Forerunner of the Messiah, Elijah.

But why does Jesus not give him a clear answer to his question? To say that He gave an evasive answer in order to test the Baptist's faith avoids the issue and has been the source of many a poor sermon. It is much simpler to assume that Jesus avoided saying either yes or no because He was not yet ready to make public who He believed Himself to be. From every point of view the account of the Baptist's question proves that at that time none of those who believed in Jesus held Him to be the Messiah. Had He already been accepted in any way as the Messiah, the Baptist would have indicated this in his question.

Another reason for finding a new interpretation came from the words of Jesus, addressed to the crowd after the

departure of the Baptist's messengers. "Among those born
of women there has risen no one greater than John the
Baptist; yet he who is least in the Kingdom of Heaven is
greater than he" (Matthew 11:11).

The usual explanation—that in these words Jesus expressed a criticism of the Baptist and placed him at a level
below that of the believers assembled round Him as adherents of the Kingdom of God—seemed to me both unsatisfying and tasteless, for these believers were also born
of women. By giving up this explanation I was forced into
the supposition that, in contrasting the Baptist with members of the Kingdom of God, Jesus was taking into account
the difference between the natural world and the supernatural Messianic world. As a man in the condition into
which all men enter at birth, the Baptist is the greatest of
all who have ever lived. But members of the Kingdom of
Heaven are no longer natural men; through the dawning
of the Messianic Kingdom they have experienced a change
that has raised them to a supernatural condition akin to
that of the angels. Because they are now supernatural
beings, the least among them is greater than the greatest
man who has ever appeared in the natural world of the age
that is now passing away. John the Baptist does, indeed,
belong to this Kingdom either as a great or a humble member of it. Yet his greatness, unique and surpassing that of
all other humans, lies in the fact that he became incarnate
in this natural world.

Thus, at the end of my first year at the university, I was
troubled by the explanation then accepted as historically
correct of the words and actions of Jesus when He sent the
disciples out on their mission. As a consequence of this, I
also questioned the interpretation that viewed the whole
life of Jesus as historical.

When I reached home after maneuvers, entirely new horizons had opened up for me. Of this I was certain: that Jesus had annouced not a kingdom that was to be founded and realized in the natural world by Himself and the believers, but one that was to be expected as coming with the approaching dawn of a supernatural age.

I would of course have considered it presumptuous to hint to Holtzmann in my examination, which I took shortly afterward, that I distrusted his conception of the life of Jesus, which was universally shared by the critical school of that time. In any case, I had no opportunity to do so. With his well-known kindness he treated me, a young student hindered in my studies by military service, so gently that in the twenty-minute interview he demanded from me nothing beyond a summary comparison of the contents of the first three Gospels.

In my remaining years at the university I pursued, often to the neglect of my other subjects, independent research on the Gospels and on the problems of the life of Jesus. Through these studies I became increasingly convinced that the key to the riddles awaiting solution is to be looked for in the explanation of the words of Jesus when He sent the disciples out on their mission, in the question sent by the Baptist from his prison, and, finally, in the way Jesus acts upon the return of the disciples.

How grateful I was that the German university does not supervise the student too closely in his studies, nor keep him breathless through constant examinations, as is the case in other countries, but offers him the opportunity for independent scholarly work!

The Strasbourg theological faculty of that day had a distinctly liberal character. Aside from Holtzmann there was

Karl Budde, the Old Testament specialist, who had recently come to Strasbourg and was my favorite theology teacher. What especially pleased me about him was his simple yet graceful presentation of his scholarly research. I found his lectures an aesthetic delight.

Along with the lectures in theology I regularly attended those in philosophy.

I studied music theory under Jacobsthal, a pupil of Bellermann, who in his one-sidedness refused to acknowledge as art any music after Beethoven's. Pure counterpoint, however, one could learn thoroughly from him, and I have much to thank him for.

In my musical development I owed much to Ernest Münch, a brother of my Mülhausen teacher, who was organist of St. Wilhelm's in Strasbourg and conductor at the Bach concerts he started with the choir of St. Wilhelm's. He entrusted to me the organ accompaniment of the cantatas and the Passion music. At first I played only at the rehearsals, in place of his Mülhausen brother, who then took my place at the actual performances. Before long, however, I also played at the performances if his brother could not come. In this way, while I was still a young student, I became familiar with the work of Bach and had an opportunity to deal with the practical problems of producing the master's cantatas and Passion music.

St. Wilhelm's Church in Strasbourg ranked at that time as one of the most important centers of the Bach renaissance that was beginning to emerge at the end of the century. Ernest Münch had an extraordinary knowledge of the works of the cantor of St. Thomas. He was one of the first to abandon the modernized rendering of the cantatas and the Passion music that had become universal at the end of the nineteenth century, and he strove for performances in a purer style, with his small choir accompanied by the famous Strasbourg orchestra. Many an evening we sat with the scores of the cantatas and the Passion music and discussed the correct method of rendering them. Ernest Münch's successor as conductor at these concerts was his son Fritz Münch, the director of the Strasbourg Conservatory.

My veneration for Bach was matched by the same feeling for Richard Wagner. When I was a schoolboy at Mülhausen, at the age of sixteen I was allowed for the first time to go to the theater, and there I heard Wagner's *Tannhäuser*. This music overpowered me to such an extent that it was days before I was capable of giving proper attention to my lessons in school.

In Strasbourg, where the operatic performances conducted by Otto Lohse were outstanding, I had the opportunity of becoming thoroughly familiar with the whole of Wagner's works, except, of course, *Parsifal*, which at that time could only be performed at Bayreuth. It was a great experience for me to be present in Bayreuth in 1896, at the memorable new performance of the tetralogy, the first since the original in 1876. Parisian friends had given me tickets. To pay for the journey I had to content myself with one meal a day.

Today, if I experience a Wagner performance with all sorts of stage effects clamoring for attention alongside the music, as though it were a film show, I cannot help thinking with regret of the earlier mise-en-scène of the tetralogy at Bayreuth, the very simplicity of which made it so marvelously effective. Not only the staging but the whole performance was in the spirit of the departed master.

Both as singer and actor Vogl, as Loge, made the deepest

impression on me. From the moment of his appearance he dominated the stage without perceptibly having to do any- thing to draw attention to himself. He did not wear the harlequin dress of modern players, nor did he dance round the stage to the rhythm of the Loge motif, as is the fashion today. The only thing about him that was striking was his red cloak. The only movements he executed to the rhythm of the music were those with which, as if acting under some compulsion, he threw his cloak now over one shoulder, now over the other, his gaze fixed on what was happening around him, yet himself quite indifferent to it all. Thus he plainly stood for the restless force of destruction among the gods, who were marching forward, blindly, to their doom.

My student years at Strasbourg passed quickly. At the end of the summer of 1897 I presented myself for the first theological examination. As the topic for the so-called thesis we were given: "A comparison of Schleiermacher's concept of the Last Supper with that of the New Testament and the professions of faith of the Reformers." The thesis was an exercise assigned to all candidates alike and had to be fin- ished within eight weeks. It determined whether one would be admitted to the examination.

This task led me back again to the problem of the Gospels and the life of Jesus. All dogmatic and historical interpre- tations of the Last Supper, which I had to review for my final examination, seemed unsatisfactory. None addressed the significance of the historical celebration of Jesus with His disciples and of the origin of the primitive Christian ceremony of the Communion. A remark of Schleiermacher in the section of his famous *Dogmatics* in which he treats the Last Supper gave me much to think about. He points out that according to the accounts of the Last Supper in Matthew and Mark, Jesus did not charge the disciples to repeat the meal. We must therefore familiarize ourselves as well as we can with the thought that the repetition of the celebration in the primitive community goes back only to the disciples and not to Jesus Himself. This thought, which Schleiermacher presented in a brilliant piece of reasoning but did not pursue to the limit of its possible historical consequences, preoccupied me even after I had completed the thesis for my candidature.

If, I said to myself, the command to repeat the meal is absent from the two oldest Gospels, that means that the disciples did in fact repeat it, with the body of believers, on their own initiative and authority. That, however, they could do only if there was something in the nature of this last meal that made it significant apart from the words and actions of Jesus. But, since no past or current explanations of the Last Supper have made intelligible how it was adopted in the primitive community without a command from Jesus, I had to conclude that the problem of the Last Supper was unresolved. Thus, I went on to investigate the question of whether the significance of the meal for Jesus and His disciples was not connected with the expectation of the Messianic feast to be celebrated in the Kingdom of God, which was soon to appear.

Paris and Berlin, 1898–1899

2

On May 6, 1898, I passed the first theological examination, the official state examination, and then spent the whole of the summer in Strasbourg to devote myself entirely to philosophy. During this time I lived in the house at the Old Fish Market (No. 36) in which Goethe had lived while he was a student at Strasbourg.

Windelband and Ziegler were eminent teachers in their subjects. Windelband's strength lay in ancient philosophy, and his seminars on Plato and Aristotle are among the best memories of my student days. Ziegler's domain was ethics and the philosophy of religion. For the latter he was especially well prepared through his earlier studies in theology at the "Stift," the Protestant seminary at Tübingen.

After my examination, at the request of Holtzmann I was given the Goll scholarship, which was administered by the St. Thomas Chapter and the theological faculty jointly. Its value was twelve hundred marks (six hundred dollars) annually, and it was awarded for six-year periods. The recipient was under an obligation either to take, in six years at the most, the degree of licentiate in theology at Strasbourg or to repay the money he had received.

On the advice of Theobald Ziegler, I determined that I would work first on a dissertation toward the doctoral degree in philosophy. At the end of the term, he suggested, in a conversation held on the steps of the University of Strasbourg under his umbrella, that my subject should be the religious philosophy of Kant, a suggestion I found most attractive. Toward the end of October 1898, I went to Paris to study philosophy at the Sorbonne, and to continue my organ lessons under Widor.

I did not attend many lectures in Paris. To begin with, the unceremonious way in which the matriculation was conducted annoyed me. The antiquated method of instruction, which made it impossible for the faculty, however outstanding in quality, to give their best, also contributed to making the Sorbonne disappointing. There were no comprehensive courses such as I had been accustomed to at Strasbourg. Either the professors gave lectures that bore solely on the examination syllabus or they lectured on special subjects.

At the Protestant theological faculty (on the Boulevard

Arago), I sometimes heard lectures on doctrine by Louis Auguste Sabatier and others by the New Testament scholar Louis Eugène Ménégoz. I felt great esteem for them both. But on the whole that winter in Paris was devoted to music and to my dissertation for the doctorate.

With Widor—who now gave me lessons without charge—I worked at the organ, and under Isidore Philipp, who a little later became a teacher at the Conservatory, at the piano. At the same time I was a pupil of Franz Liszt's talented pupil and friend Marie Jaëll-Trautmann, an Alsatian by birth. She had already retired from a life of public piano recitals, at which, for a short time, she shone as a star of the first magnitude. She now dedicated herself to the study of the physiological aspects of piano playing. I was the guinea pig on which she tried her experiments, which were made in cooperation with the physiologist Féré, so I participated in them. How much I owe to this gifted woman!

The finger—so her theory goes—must be as fully conscious as possible of its relationship to the keys. The player must be conscious of the tension and of the relaxation of the muscles from the shoulder down to the fingertips. He must learn to prevent all involuntary and all unconscious movements. Finger exercises that aim merely at rapidity must be renounced. As the finger prepares for a motion, it must always try to project the desired sound. A resonant touch is realized by the quickest and lightest possible depression of the keys. But the finger must also be conscious of the way it lets the depressed key rise again. In the depression and releasing of the keys the finger finds itself in an imperceptibly rolling movement, either inward (toward the thumb) or outward (toward the little finger). When several keys are depressed one after another, with movements rolling in the same direction, the corresponding tones and chords are organically linked.

Tones produced by movements that roll in different directions stay apart by their very nature. Through thoughtfully differentiated movements of the fingers and of the hand, one can attain both differentiation of sonority and sensitivity to phrasing. To achieve an ever more conscious and ever closer relationship with the keys, the finger must cultivate to the utmost its sensitivity to their touch. With the perfecting of this sensitivity the player will become at the same time more responsive both to tone color and to color in general.

Marie Jaëll pushed this theory to the extreme by proclaiming that through the appropriate development of the hand nonmusical people could become musical. Starting from the physiology of the piano touch, she wanted to advance a theory about the nature of art in general. She thus obscured her correct and forceful observations about the essence of artful touch with deep, often baroque-sounding observations and deprived herself of the recognition her research deserved.

Under Marie Jaëll's guidance I completely transformed my hand. I owe it to her that by well-directed, time-saving practice I became increasingly master of my fingers to the great benefit of my organ playing.

The more traditional piano instruction I received from Philipp was also extraordinarily valuable and protected me from what was one-sided in the Jaell method. As my two teachers had a poor opinion of each other, I had to keep each from knowing that I was a pupil of the other. What trouble it cost me to play with Marie Jaëll in the morning à la Jaëll and with Philipp in the afternoon à la Philipp!

With Philipp and Widor I am still united in a firm bond of friendship; Marie Jaëll died in 1925. Through Widor I met many interesting personalities in the Paris of that day. He was also concerned about my material welfare. Many a time, if he had the impression that my slender purse did not provide me with enough to eat adequately, he took me after my lesson to his regular haunt, the Restaurant Foyot near the Luxembourg, so I might have a satisfying meal.

My father's two brothers and their wives, who had settled in Paris, also showed me much kindness. The younger one, Charles, who had made a name for himself as a linguist through his efforts to improve the teaching of modern languages, put me in touch with people at the university. Thus I was able to feel at home in Paris.

My thesis for the doctorate suffered in no way from the demands made on me, either by my art or by my social life, for my good health allowed me to be prodigal with nocturnal labor. It happened sometimes that I played for Widor in the morning without having been to bed at all.

To consult the literature on Kant's philosophy of religion in the Bibliothèque Nationale proved to be impracticable because of the cumbersome regulations in the reading room. I therefore resolved without further ado to write the thesis without troubling about the literature, and to see what results I could obtain by burying myself in the Kantian writings themselves.

As I studied these texts, I noticed variations in his use of language; for example, in several passages on religious issues in his *Critique of Pure Reason* the word *intelligible*, which corresponds to Kant's basic criticism, is replaced by the more naive term *transcendental*. I then traced all expressions of significance throughout his works on the philosophy of religion in order to find the context in which they appear, and to see whether they had undergone some change in meaning. This enabled me to prove that the long section on the "Canon of Pure Reason" is not a part of the *Critique of Pure Reason*, but actually an earlier work of Kant that he included there, although it does not agree with what came later. The earlier study he called "A Sketch of the Philosophy of Religion."

Another discovery was that Kant never developed any further the religiophilosophical scheme of transcendental dialectic found in the *Critique of Pure Reason*. His religious philosophy in the *Critique of Practical Reason*, with its three postulates of God, Freedom, and Immortality, is not at all the same as that hinted at in the *Critique of Pure Reason*. In the *Critique of Judgment* and in *Religion Within the Limits of Reason Alone*, he abandoned the religious philosophy of the three postulates. The train of thought that appears in these later works leads one back once more to the path taken in the "Sketch of the Philosophy of Religion."

Kant's philosophy of religion, then, which everyone regarded as identical to that of the three postulates, is in fact constantly changing. This is because the presuppositions of his critical idealism and the religiophilosophical claims of the moral law are incompatible. In Kant's work his critical and his ethical philosophies of religion developed in tandem, as he sought to adjust and reconcile both. In the transcendental dialectic of the *Critique of Pure Reason* he thought he had unified them without difficulty. But the scheme he designed does not work because Kant, rather than staying with his earlier concept of the moral law, as prefigured in the transcendental dialectic of the *Critique of Pure Reason*, enriches it constantly. This more profound conception of moral law raises religious questions, however, which go beyond what can be found in Kant's conception of religious idealism. At the point where his religious philosophy acquires its more profound moral law, it loses its interest in the very convictions that occupy the foremost place in critical idealism; significantly in this connection, when Kant's religious thought is most completely dominated by his deepest ethic, the postulate of Immortality plays no part. Instead, then, of keeping to the philosophy of religion established by critical idealism, Kant allows himself to be led further away from it by the religious philosophy of his ever deepening moral law. As he becomes more profound, he is unable to remain consistent.

In the middle of March 1899, I returned to Strasbourg and presented my completed study to Theobald Ziegler. He approved it and scheduled the defense of my dissertation for the end of July.

I spent the summer of 1899 in Berlin, mainly occupied with reading philosophy. My goal was to have read all the chief works of ancient and modern philosophy. At the same time I attended lectures by Harnack, Pfleiderer, Kaftan, Paulsen, and Simmel. At Simmel's lectures I was at first an occasional, but afterward a regular, auditor.

It was only later that I established contact with Harnack, whose *History of Dogma* I had read in Strasbourg with great enthusiasm. I had been introduced to him by friends, and I visited his home. I was so overawed by his knowledge and the universality of his interests that I was too inhibited to answer his questions adequately when he spoke to me. Later in life I received from him many postcards, cordial and full of substance. The postcard was his usual means of correspondence. Two very detailed cards that I received at Lambaréné about my then just published book, *The Mysticism of Paul the Apostle*, belong to the year 1930 and must be among the last that he ever wrote.

I spent a great deal of time with Carl Stumpf. His psychological studies on auditory sensitivity were of great interest to me. I participated regularly in the experiments he and his assistants performed, and again I served as guinea pig, as I had done with Marie Jaëll in Strasbourg.

The Berlin organists, with the exception of Egidi, disappointed me somewhat because they were more interested in virtuosity than in the true plasticity of style to which Widor attached so much importance. And how dull and dry was the sound of the new Berlin organs compared with that of Cavaillé-Col's instruments in St. Sulpice and Notre Dame.

Professor Heinrich Reimann, the organist of the Kaiser Wilhelm Memorial Church, to whom I had brought a letter of introduction from Widor, allowed me to play the organ regularly, and engaged me as his deputy when he went away on holiday. Thanks to him I made the acquaintance of some of the musicians, painters, and sculptors of Berlin.

I became acquainted with the academic world at the home of the widow of Ernst Curtius, the well-known Hellenist. She received me cordially as an acquaintance of her stepson, the district superintendent of Colmar. There I often met Hermann Grimm, who tried hard to convert me from the heresy that the contents of the fourth Gospel are not reconcilable with those of the first three. To this day I consider it my great good fortune that I had the privilege of meeting the leaders of intellectual life of the Berlin of that day.

The intellectual life of Berlin made a much greater impression on me than that of Paris. In Paris, the cosmopolitan city, the intellectual life was fragmented. One had to get thoroughly acclimatized before one could see its merits. The intellectual life of Berlin, in contrast, had its center in its well-organized, lively university. Moreover, Berlin at that time was not yet a cosmopolitan city but gave the impression of being a provincial town that was developing happily in every respect. Altogether it had an air of healthy self-assurance and a confident faith in its destiny not to be found in contemporary Paris, which was then being torn apart by the Dreyfus case. Thus I came to know and love Berlin during the finest period of its existence. I was especially impressed by the simple life-style of Berlin society and the ease with which one was admitted to its families.

The First Years in
Strasbourg

3

At the end of July 1899, I returned to Strasbourg to receive my doctorate in philosophy. In the oral examination, Ziegler and Windelband both thought that I fell below the level my dissertation had led them to expect from me. The time I had spent with Stumpf in his experiments had been lost so far as preparation for the examination was concerned. In addition, in reading original works I had neglected my textbooks far too much.

The dissertation appeared as a book before the end of 1899 under the title *The Religious Philosophy of Kant:*

From the "Critique of Pure Reason" to "Religion Within the Limits of Reason Alone."

Theobald Ziegler advised me to qualify as a privatdozent in the philosophy faculty, but I decided for theology. He hinted to me that if I were a privatdozent in philosophy people would not be pleased to see me active as a preacher as well. But to me preaching was an inner necessity. The opportunity to speak every Sunday to a congregation about the essential questions of life seemed to me wonderful.

From this time on I remained in Strasbourg. Although I was no longer a student, I was given permission to live in the Collegium Wilhelmitanum (the seminary of St. Thomas), which I loved so well. The room overlooking the quiet garden with its big trees—the room in which I had passed so many happy hours as a student—seemed a most appropriate place for the work that now lay before me.

The moment I had finished correcting the proofs of my doctoral dissertation, I set to work on getting my licentiate to teach theology. I decided to obtain that degree as quickly as I could so that the Goll fellowship I held could be made available to another qualified student as soon as possible. My friend Jäger, a gifted student of Oriental languages, for whose sake I hastened, never made use of this fellowship. Instead he became director of the Protestant Gymnasium at Strasbourg. Had I known this I would have traveled longer before settling down, and would also have studied at some English universities.

On December 1, 1899, I obtained a post as assistant vicar of the Church of St. Nicholai in Strasbourg. Later, after I had passed the second theological examination, I was appointed vicar. This second examination, usually conducted by elderly clerics, I barely passed on July 15, 1900. So occupied was I with the dissertation for the theological licentiate, I had neglected to refresh my memory as I should have on the various branches of theology, which this examination demanded. It was only through the forceful intervention of Pfarrer Will, whom I had delighted with my knowledge of the history of dogma, that I did not fail. It was especially unfortunate that I did not know enough about the hymn writers and their lives.

The staff at St. Nicholai consisted of two elderly, but still vigorous, ministers: Pastor Knittel, one of my father's predecessors at Günsbach, and Pastor Gerold, an intimate friend of one of my mother's brothers, who had been incumbent at St. Nicholai but had died young. To these two men I was appointed as an assistant, chiefly so that I might relieve them of the afternoon service, the Sunday children's service, and the confirmation classes.

The tasks given to me were a constant source of joy. At the afternoon service, with only a small group of worshipers present, I could use the intimate style of preaching I had inherited from my father and in which I could express myself better than at the morning service. Even today I am never quite free from shyness before a large audience. As the years passed, the two old gentlemen had to spare themselves more and more, and I frequently had to preach in the morning as well. I used to write my sermons out in full, often making two or three drafts before I had the final version. When delivering the sermons, however, I did not tie myself to this text, which I had carefully memorized, but often departed from it considerably.

My afternoon sermons, which I looked upon as simple devotional meditations rather than sermons, were so short that on one occasion certain circles of the congregation complained. Pastor Knittel, who also held the office of "Inspector of Spiritual Matters," had to call me before him, and when I appeared he was as embarrassed as I was.

To his question as to how he should respond to the aggrieved members of the congregation, I answered that he might reply that I was only a poor curate who stopped speaking when he found he had nothing more to say about the text. Thereupon he dismissed me with a mild reprimand and an admonition not to preach for less than twenty minutes.

Pastor Knittel represented orthodoxy softened by pietism; Pastor Gerold was a liberal. But they fulfilled the duties of their office together in a truly brotherly spirit. Everything was carried out in perfect harmony. The work accomplished at this unpretentious church, opposite the St. Thomas seminary, was remarkable.

Many times during these years, whenever I had a free Sunday, I went to Günsbach to take over the service for my father. Three times a week, from eleven to twelve, when the morning lessons were over, I had to take up the confirmation classes for boys. I tried hard to give them as little homework as possible, so that the lessons might be a time of pure enjoyment for heart and spirit. I therefore used the last ten minutes of our classes to recite with them words from the Bible and verses from hymns, so that they would know them and the words would stay with them throughout their lives. The aim of my teaching was to bring to their hearts and thoughts the great truths of the Gospels so religion would have meaning in their lives and give them the strength to resist the irreligious forces that might assail them. I also tried to awaken in them a love for the Church, and a desire for that hour of spiritual peace to be found in

the Sunday service. I taught them to respect traditional
doctrines, but at the same time to hold fast to the saying
of Paul that where the spirit of Christ is, there is freedom.

Of the seeds that for years I was thus sowing, some have
taken root and grown, as I have been privileged to learn.
Men have thanked me for having then brought home to
their hearts the fundamental truths of the religion of Jesus
as something not hostile to reason, but, on the contrary,
as strengthening them. This has helped them to keep their
religion later in life.

In these classes of religious instruction I first became
conscious of how much of the schoolmaster's blood I had
in me from my ancestors.

My stipend at St. Nicholai was one hundred marks (fifty
dollars) a month, but it sufficed for my needs, as my board
and lodging at the St. Thomas hostel were very cheap.

One great advantage of my position there was that it left
me plenty of time for scholarly pursuits and for music. The
thoughtfulness of the two ministers made it possible for me
to leave Strasbourg when the children were on their spring
and fall vacations. I had only to provide for a substitute
preacher, and when nobody else was available, they were
kind enough to preach themselves. Thus I had three months
out of the year free, one after Easter and two in the fall.
The spring holiday I usually spent in Paris in order to
continue my studies with Widor. The autumn I spent for
the most part in my parents' home at Günsbach.

During these extended visits to Paris I made many valuable acquaintances. Romain Rolland I met for the first

time around 1905, and in the beginning we were merely musicians to each other. Gradually, however, we discovered that we were humans too, and we became good friends.

With Henri Lichtenberger, the sensitive French connoisseur of German literature, I developed a warm friendship. Robert Minder, my student in music and philosophy, became his successor in Strasbourg after 1918.

I shall never forget a chance encounter I had one delightful spring morning at the beginning of the century in the narrow rue St.-Jacques. As I was late for an appointment, I had to take a cab. At one street crossing the two lines of vehicles had to remain stationary side by side for some time, and I was attracted by the head of the occupant of the open carriage alongside mine. I noticed that the elegant tall hat—at that time the tall hat was still worn in Paris—looked odd upon the anything-but-elegant head. But while I continued to look—for we had to wait a considerable time—I fell under the spell of the uncanny something, which was the very reverse of spiritual, that characterized the face. Such indications of untamed primitive human nature, features expressing reckless and remorseless willpower, I had never seen before in any human being. While I was staring, it suddenly dawned on me that it was Clemenceau.

When I learned later that after three sittings Cézanne had given up the task of painting Clemenceau because he "couldn't make a portrait of a thing like that," I thoroughly understood what he meant.

During the first years of the new century I delivered a series of lectures, in German, on German literature and philosophy before the Foreign Language Society of Paris.

I still remember those on Nietzsche, Schopenhauer, Gerhart Hauptmann, Sudermann, and Goethe's *Faust*. In August 1900, while I was working on the lecture on Nietzsche, the news came that death had at last released him from his sufferings.

My life was simple in those years, which were decisive for my creative work. I worked a great deal, with unbroken concentration but without haste.

I did not travel much, because I had neither the time nor the money. In 1900 I accompanied my aunt, the wife of my father's eldest brother, to Oberammergau. The wonderful landscape behind the stage actually made a stronger impression on me than the Passion play. I was bothered by the staging of the essential action of the Passion in pictorial scenes from the Old Testament, by the excessively theatrical display, by the imperfections of the text, and by the banality of the music. What touched me deeply was the pious fervor with which the actors immersed themselves in the parts they played.

We cannot help but feel dissatisfied with a Passion play that was meant to be performed, using simple methods, by villagers for villagers and as a religious service, but is forced out of this mold by a flood of foreign spectators and turned into a stage play that must satisfy the demands of all those who see it. Anyone sensitive to the spiritual side of life must admit that the people of Oberammergau make every effort to perform this Passion play, even with its changes, in the simple spirit in which it was originally conceived.

When my finances permitted, I made the pilgrimage to Bayreuth in those years the festival took place. Cosima Wagner, whom I had met in Strasbourg while working on my book on Bach, made a deep impression on me. She became interested in my idea that Bach's music is descriptive. Once, when she visited the eminent church historian Johannes Ficker in Strasbourg, she asked me to illustrate my view by playing some of Bach's choral preludes on the fine Merklin organ in the new church. She also, on that occasion, gave me interesting details about the religious instruction she had received in her youth and later, after she had decided to convert to Protestantism. However often we met I was never able to overcome my shyness in the presence of this noble, highly artistic, extraordinary woman.

In Siegfried Wagner I valued the simplicity and the modesty that characterized this man so very talented in so many fields. No one who saw him at work in Bayreuth could help but admire him, both for what he did and for the way in which he did it. His music too contains much that is truly significant and beautiful.

Study of the Last Supper and the Life of Jesus, 1900–1902

4

After finishing my work on Kant, when I returned to theology it would have been natural for me to take up my studies of the problems of the life of Jesus, which had occupied me since my first student days. I could have gathered the material and developed it into a dissertation. My studies of the Last Supper had, however, broadened my views and my interests. The research on the life of Jesus had led me to research on primitive Christianity. The problem of the Last Supper belongs, of course, to both of these subjects. It stands at the center of the development of the faith of Jesus and of primitive Christianity.

If, I said to myself, the origin and significance of the Last Supper remain an enigma for us, we apparently do not understand the world of thought of the times of Jesus and of early Christianity. In addition, we cannot grasp the real problems of the faith of Jesus and of primitive Christianity because we do not regard them as based on the Last Supper and baptism.

Guided by these considerations, I conceived the idea of writing a history of the Last Supper as it related both to the life of Jesus and to the history of primitive Christianity. A preliminary investigation was meant to define my position regarding previous research into the question of the Last Supper and to throw light upon the problem as a whole. A second part would describe the thought and activities of Jesus as conditions for understanding the last supper that He celebrated with His disciples. A third part was to treat the Last Supper in the primitive Church and in the first two centuries of Christianity.

For my work on the problem of the Last Supper, I obtained my degree in theology (the diploma of licentiate in theology) on July 21, 1900. Its second part, on the mystery of the Messiahship and the Passion, served as qualification to teach as privatdozent at the university in 1902.

When the third study, devoted to the Last Supper in primitive Christianity, and the fourth, on the history of baptism in the New Testament and primitive Christianity, were completed, I used them in my course lectures. Neither has been published. *The Quest of the Historical Jesus*, which I originally considered a supplement to a sketch on the life of Jesus, grew into a large volume and prevented the preparation of other studies for publication.

After this came a new interruption: the book on Bach and, after that, my medical studies. When, near the conclusion of these studies, I could find time once more to devote to theology, I decided to write a history of scholarly research into the thought of the Apostle Paul. This would then be a companion volume to *The Quest of the Historical Jesus* and an introduction to an exposition of Pauline doctrine.

On the strength of my newly won understanding of the teachings of Jesus and Paul, I intended to complete a history of the origin and early development of Christianity and the Last Supper and baptism. I had planned to do this after my first stay in Africa, when, after one and a half or two years, I would have leave in Europe. This plan, however, was ruined by the war, which only allowed me to return to Europe after four and a half years in Africa, and then in bad health and deprived of my livelihood.

In the meantime another project interfered: I had begun to work on *The Philosophy of Civilization*. Consequently, "The History of the Last Supper and Baptism in the Early Christian Period" has remained in manuscript form for my lectures. The thoughts that underlie it are put forward in my book *The Mysticism of Paul the Apostle*.

In my work on the problem of the Last Supper I examined the various solutions that had been offered by theologians up to the end of the nineteenth century. At the same time I attempted to reveal its true character. In the course of my studies it became evident that the solutions offered to explain the early Christian celebration of the distribution of bread and wine are impossible. Repetition of the words of Jesus cannot turn bread and wine into His body and blood.

The celebration as practiced in early Christendom was something other than a sacramental repetition or symbolical representation of the atoning death of Jesus. That interpretation of the last meal of Jesus with His disciples was added much later, in the Catholic Mass and in the Protestant celebration of the Last Supper, as a symbol of the forgiveness of sins.

The words of Jesus about bread and wine as His body and blood did not—strange as the statement may seem to us—determine the nature of the celebration for the disciples and the first believers. According to our knowledge of primitive Christianity, those words were not repeated at the community meal in the beginning. What constituted the celebration, then, was not Jesus' words of the so-called institution, which spoke of bread and wine as His body and blood, but the prayers of thanksgiving over the bread and wine. These gave both to the last supper of Jesus with His disciples and to the solemn meal of the early Christian community a meaning that pointed toward the expected Messianic meal.

This explains why the celebration of the Last Supper is called "Eucharist," that is, a "Thanksgiving." It was celebrated not once a year on the evening of Maundy Thursday but in the early hours every Sunday, to signify the day of the resurrection of Jesus, when believers looked forward to His return and the coming of the Kingdom of God.

In the sketch on the life of Jesus, published under the title *The Secret of Jesus' Messiahship and Passion*, I presented the nineteenth-century views of the early public activities and sermons of Jesus. These were accepted as historically authentic, and were confirmed in detail by Holtzmann in his work on the Gospels. His views are based upon two fundamental ideas: first, that Jesus did not share the naive, realistic expectation of the return of the Messiah, which was at that time widespread among the Jewish people; and that it was owing to the failures He experienced after some initial successes that He decided to submit to His suffering and death.

Theological scholarship of the second half of the nineteenth century held that Jesus tries to divert the attention of believers from the supernatural Messianic Kingdom they expect by proclaiming an ethical Kingdom of God in this world. Accordingly, He does not hold Himself to be the Messiah of His hearers' imagination but tries to instill in them a belief in a spiritual, ethical Messiah, who will enable them to recognize the Messiah in Him.

At first His preaching was successful. Later on, however, the multitude, influenced by the Pharisees and the rulers at Jerusalem, falls away from Him. As he realizes this, he accepts that it is the will of God that, for the sake of the Kingdom of God and in order to establish His own spiritual Messiahship, he must die. Thus the next Easter he travels to Jerusalem to surrender Himself to suffering and death on the cross.

This view of the thought and decisions of Jesus is untenable, because its two fundamental ideas do not correspond to facts. Nowhere in the oldest sources, the Gospels of Mark and Matthew, is there any indication that Jesus wanted to replace the realistic view of a future supernatural Kingdom of God, as it was held by the people of that time, with a spiritualized Kingdom. Nor do those Gospels say anything about a successful period of activity being followed by an unsuccessful one.

As shown by the sayings Mark and Matthew ascribe to Him, Jesus lives in the Messianic expectation, held by late Judaism, that goes back to the old prophets and to the Book of Daniel, a book which came into existence around 165 B.C. We know of this expectation from the Book of Enoch (ca. 100 B.C.), the Psalms of Solomon (63 B.C.), and the Apocalypses of Baruch and Ezra (ca. A.D. 80).

Like His contemporaries, Jesus identifies the Messiah with the "Son of Man," who is mentioned in the Book of Daniel, and who speaks of His coming on the clouds of heaven. The Kingdom of God He preaches is the heavenly Messianic Kingdom, which will be established on earth when the Son of Man comes at the end of the natural world. He constantly exhorts His listeners to be ready at any moment for the judgment, as a result of which some will enter into the glory of the Messianic Kingdom while others will face damnation. He even offers His disciples the prospect of sitting, at this judgment, on twelve seats around His throne and judging the twelve tribes of Israel.

Jesus accepts, then, as true the late Jewish Messianic expectation in all its realistic aspects. In no way does He attempt to spiritualize it. But He fills it with His own powerful ethical spirit, passing beyond the Law and the scribes. He demands from men the practice of the absolute ethic of love as proof that they belong to God and to the Messiah and will be elected to membership in the coming Kingdom. In the Sermon on the Mount he announces who is predestined to receive future blessings: the simple, the merciful, the peacemakers, the pure in heart, those who hunger and thirst after the justice of the Kingdom of God, the mourners, those who suffer persecution for the Kingdom of God's sake, those who become as little children.

The error of earlier research is that it attributes to Jesus a spiritualizing of the late Jewish Messianic expectation, whereas in reality He simply introduces into it the ethical religion of love. Our minds refuse at first to grasp that a religiousness and an ethic so deep and spiritual can be combined with other views so naively realistic. But the combination is a fact.

Against the hypothesis that there are two phases in the activity of Jesus, a successful period and an unsuccessful, we can point to the fact that in His last period in Galilee, as well as at the Temple in Jerusalem, enthusiastic crowds gathered around Him. Surrounded by his followers, He is protected against His enemies. With their support He can even venture in His discourses at the Temple to attack the Pharisees, and to drive the traders and the money changers out of it.

When, after the return of the disciples whom He had sent on a mission to proclaim the coming of the Kingdom of God, He goes with them to the heathen region of Tyre and Sidon, He is not motivated by a need to withdraw from His enemies. The people do not leave Him; on the contrary, He retires to have some time alone with those closest to Him. As soon as He appears again in Galilee, the crowd of His adherents gathers round Him. It is at the head of the Galilean pilgrims on their way to the Easter celebration that He enters Jerusalem. His arrest and crucifixion are only possible because He Himself surrenders to the authorities. They condemn Him during the night, and in the early morning, almost before Jerusalem is awake, he is already crucified.

Following the precise statements of the two oldest Gospels, I counter the untenable earlier interpretations of the life of Jesus with a new concept: I show that His thought, word, and action were based on His expectation that the end of the world was near and that the Kingdom of God would be revealed. This interpretation is called "eschatological" (from the Greek word *eschatos*, meaning "the last") and it is in accordance with the traditional Jewish-Christian doctrine concerning the events leading to the end of the world.

If we look at the life of Jesus in this way—and we must remember that our factual knowledge is limited to His public appearances and His end—then we see the following: Just as Jesus announces the Kingdom of God not as something already beginning but as something of the future, He does not think that He is already the Messiah. He is convinced that only at the appearance of the Messianic Kingdom, when those predestined enter the supernatural existence intended for them, will He be manifested as the Messiah. This knowledge about His future dignity remains His secret. To the people He presents Himself only as the One who announces the imminent coming of the Kingdom of God. His listeners do not have to know who He is. When the Kingdom of God comes, they will realize it. The knowledge of who He is has manifested itself only to those who recognize Him, as the disciples have done, and who accept His message of the Kingdom of God. He promises that the Son of Man (to whom He refers in the third person, as if He were not identical with Him) will recognize them immediately as His own.

For Himself and those who look with Him for the imminent coming of the Kingdom of God, Jesus expects that they will first have to endure together the pre-Messianic Tribulation and then prove themselves faithful. For according to the late Jewish teaching about events at the end of the world, all those who are called to the Messianic Kingdom will, immediately before this takes place, suffer for some time at the mercy of the God-opposing powers of this world.

At some point in time—whether it was weeks or months after His appearance in public we do not know—Jesus feels certain that the hour for the coming of the Kingdom has arrived. He hastily sends out His disciples two by two into the cities of Israel that they may spread the news. In the instructions he gives them (Matthew 10), He warns them to expect the Messianic Tribulation which is immediately about to dawn and bring upon them and the other elect ones fierce persecution, yes, perhaps death itself. He does not expect to see them return to Him but assures them that the "coming of the Son of Man" (which is expected to be simultaneous with the manifestation of the Kingdom) will take place even before they have visited all the cities of Israel.

His expectation, however, is not fulfilled. The disciples return without having suffered any persecution whatever. Of the pre-Messianic Tribulation there is no sign, and the Messianic Kingdom does not appear. Jesus can explain this fact to Himself only by supposing that there is still some event that must take place first.

The perception dawns on Him that the Kingdom of God can only come when He, as the Messiah-to-be, has by suffering and death made atonement for those who have been elected to the Kingdom, and thereby saved them from the necessity of going through the pre-Messianic Tribulation.

Jesus has always counted on the possibility that God, in His mercy, might spare the elect the pre-Messianic suffering. In the Lord's Prayer, which is a prayer about the coming of the Kingdom of God, believers are bidden to pray that God not lead them into "temptation" but deliver them from "Evil." By this "temptation" Jesus does not mean any individual temptation to commit sin. He refers to the persecution that will take place, with the authorization of God, at the end of time. Believers will have to suffer this at the hands of "the Evil One," Satan, who represents the powers that oppose God.

The thought, then, with which Jesus meets death is that God is willing to accept His self-chosen death as an atonement made for believers. In this way the believers do not suffer the pre-Messianic tribulations in which through suffering and death they would be purified and prove themselves worthy to enter the Kingdom of God.

The resolution of Jesus to suffer an atoning death is also based upon the passages in Isaiah about the Servant of Jehovah (Isaiah 53) who suffers for the sins of others without their understanding the significance of what He endures. Originally, these passages from Isaiah, from the period of the Jewish exile, referred to the suffering inflicted on Israel by other people at that time. By enduring their suffering as "Servants of God," the people of Israel would then bring other people to recognize the true God.

When Jesus and His disciples were in the area of Caesarea Philippi, He reveals to them the necessity of suffering and death for Him who was destined to be the Messiah. At the same time He discloses to them that He is "the Son of Man" (Mark 8:27-33). Then at Eastertime He goes up with the crowds of Galileans to Jerusalem. The rejoicing at His entry into Jerusalem is not for the Messiah but for the prophet of Nazareth, of the House of David. The treason of Judas consists not in betraying to the Sanhedrin where Jesus can be arrested but in disclosing His claim to be the Messiah.

At the last supper He takes with His disciples, He gives them to eat and to drink bread and wine that He has consecrated by prayers of thanksgiving. He declares that He will no longer drink of the fruit of the vine until that day when He will drink it again in His Father's Kingdom. Thus at His last earthly meal He blesses them as His companions at the coming Messianic meal. From that time onward believers carry within them the assurance that they are invited to the Messianic meal, and gather together for ceremonial meals with food and drink and prayers of thanksgiving.

Through this continuation of the Last Supper they hope to hasten the coming of the Kingdom of God. Jesus, then, expects that through his atoning death the Messianic Kingdom will come about without any preliminary suffering. He tells His judges that they will see Him as the Son of Man seated on the right hand of God and coming on the clouds of heaven (Mark 14:62). Since on the morning after the Sabbath the disciples find the grave empty and, in their enthusiastic expectation of the glory in which their Master is soon to appear, have visions of Him risen from the grave, they are certain that He is with God in heaven, and that he will soon appear as the Messiah and usher in the Kingdom of God.

What the two oldest Gospels report of the public life of Jesus takes place in the course of one year. In the spring, with the parable of the sower, Jesus begins to proclaim the secret of the Kingdom of God. At harvesttime He is hoping that the heavenly harvest, like the earthly one, will begin and He sends out the disciples to make a final proclamation of the nearness of the Kingdom (Matthew 9:37ff.). Shortly after that, He abandons His public activity and retires with His disciples to heathen territory in the neighborhood of Caesarea Philippi, probably until around Easter, when He joins a group of pilgrims from Galilee on their journey to Jerusalem. It is possible, then, that the period of His public activity lasted at most five or six months.

Teaching Activities at the University of Strasbourg.
The Quest of the Historical Jesus

5

On March 1, 1902, I delivered my inaugural lecture before the theological faculty at Strasbourg on the Logos doctrine in the fourth Gospel.

Later I learned that protests against my acceptance as a university lecturer had been lodged by two members of the faculty. They expressed disapproval of my method of historical investigation and fear that I should confuse the students with my views. They were not successful, however, as they could not stand up to the authority of Holtzmann, who took my side.

In the inaugural lecture, I showed that the obscure passages in the discourses of the Johannine Christ hang together, though they do not become intelligible until they are recognized as being indications by which Christ prepares His hearers to accept the sacraments as deriving their power from the Logos. Only later did I have an opportunity to develop this theory fully in my book *The Mysticism of Paul the Apostle*.

In the summer term of 1902, I began my lectures with a course on the Epistles of Timothy and Titus, the so-called pastoral Epistles.

The inspiration for studying the history of research into the life of Jesus came from a conversation with students who had attended a course of lectures by Professor Spitta on the life of Jesus, but who knew practically nothing about previous research on the subject. I therefore resolved, with Professor Holtzmann's approval, to lecture for two hours weekly during the summer term of 1905 on the history of research on the life of Jesus. I began the task with great zeal. The subject soon captivated me so completely that I devoted all my energy to its pursuit. Thanks to bequests from Edouard Reuss and other Strasbourg theologians, the university library possessed a virtually complete collection of literature on the life of Jesus. In addition, the library held nearly all the controversial writings provoked by the publications of Strauss's and Renan's lives. There was hardly another place in the world where circumstances could have been so favorable for studying the history of research on the life of Jesus.

While I was engaged in this work, I was director of the Collegium Wilhelmitanum (the seminary of St. Thomas). Immediately after the death of Erichson, I had been made acting director for the period May 1 to September 30, 1901, when Gustav Anrich—at that time pastor at Lingolsheim near Strasbourg—would take over those duties. In the summer of 1903, however, Anrich was appointed professor of Church History as successor to Ernst Lucius, who had died suddenly, so on October 1, 1903, I was in turn appointed director and given the beautiful quarters overlooking the sunny St. Thomas embankment and a yearly stipend of two thousand marks. For my study I kept the old room I had occupied as a student. While Gustav Anrich had been director, I had lived in town.

The Quest of the Historical Jesus appeared as early as 1906, the first edition bearing the subtitle *From Reimarus to Wrede*.

Hermann Samuel Reimarus (1694–1768) was professor of Oriental languages at Hamburg. His treatise *The Aims of Jesus and His Disciples* was the first attempt to explain the life of Christ based on the hypothesis that Jesus shared the eschatological Messianic expectations of his contemporaries. The treatise was first published by Lessing after the death of Reimarus as *Wolfenbüttler Fragmente* without mentioning the author's name.

William Wrede (1859–1907), professor of theology at Breslau, in his treatise *The Messianic Secret of the Gospels* made the first solid attempt to deny that Jesus entertained any eschatological ideas at all. From there, he was led to the further assumption that Jesus did not regard himself as the Messiah and that his disciples did not proclaim Him as such until after His death.

Since Reimarus and Wrede represent the two poles of

my research, I chose their names for the subtitle of my book.

After I had worked through the numerous lives of Jesus, I found it very difficult to organize them into chapters. After vain attempts to do this on paper, I piled all the "lives" in one big heap in the middle of my room, selected a place for each of the chapters in a corner or between the pieces of furniture, and then, after considerable thought, sorted the volumes into the piles to which they belonged. I pledged myself to find a place for every book in some pile, and then to leave each heap undisturbed in its place until the corresponding chapter in the manuscript was finished. I followed this plan to the very end. For many months people who visited me had to thread their way across the room along paths that ran between heaps of books. I had also to ensure that the tidying zeal of the trusty Württemberg widow who kept house for me halted before it reached the piles of books.

The first representatives of the historical-critical method who pursued research into the life of Jesus had to struggle with the task of exploring the existence of Jesus using purely historical means and to examine critically the Gospels that served as sources of information. Gradually they came to recognize that Jesus' understanding of His mission could be researched through a historical and critical analysis of the available information about His teaching and His deeds.

The lives of Jesus written in the eighteenth and early nineteenth centuries depict Jesus as the Master who enlightens His people and seeks to lead them from the nonspiritual religion of the Jews to a faith in the God of love and a spiritual Kingdom of God that is established on this earth through the Messiah. They endeavor to explain all the miracles of Jesus as natural events misunderstood by the multitude, and thus they try to put an end to all belief in the miraculous. The most famous of these rationalistic lives of Jesus is that of Karl Heinrich Venturini: *A Non-Supernatural History of the Great Prophet of Nazareth*, which in the years 1800 to 1802 appeared anonymously in German at "Bethlehem" (in reality Copenhagen) in four volumes comprising twenty-seven hundred pages. No one of that period took any notice at all of the attempt Reimarus made to understand the preaching of Jesus from the standpoint of the eschatological Messianic doctrine of late Judaism.

Genuine historical research begins with critical analysis of the Gospels to determine the historical value of their accounts. This effort, which began in the nineteenth century and continued for several decades, had the following results: The picture given by the Gospel of John is irreconcilable with that of the other three; the other three are the older and therefore the more credible sources; the material they have in common with one another is found in its earliest form in the Gospel of Mark; and, finally, Luke's Gospel is considerably later than those of Mark and Matthew.

Research into the life of Jesus found itself in a difficult situation when David Friedrich Strauss (1808–1874), in his *Life of Jesus*, published in 1835, accepted only a small portion of what the two oldest Gospels report about Jesus. According to him, most of the accounts are of a mythical character, which gradually came into existence in primitive Christianity. Most of these narratives go back to passages relating to the Messiah in the Old Testament.

Finally, when Strauss questions the credibility of the two oldest narratives, it is not because he is by nature a skeptic. He does so because he is the first to realize how difficult it is to understand the details the Evangelists give of Jesus' public life and preaching.

From the middle of the nineteenth century onward, a modern historical view gradually developed, holding that Jesus attempted to spiritualize the realistic Messianic hopes of contemporary Judaism by coming forward as a spiritual Messiah and founder of an ethical Kingdom of God. When He saw that the people did not understand Him and withdrew, He resolved to die for His cause, and in this way to carry it to victory.

Of the presentations of the life of Jesus that share this concept, the best known are those of Ernest Renan (1863), Theodore Keim (three volumes, 1867; 1871; 1872), Karl Hase (1876), and Oscar Holtzmann (1901). Heinrich Julius Holtzmann attempted to provide a scholarly basis for this interpretation in his books on the first three Gospels. The most lively presentation of this modernized theory about Jesus is to be found in Harnack's *What Is Christianity?* (1901).

As early as 1860 the various investigations into the problems of the life of Jesus began to make it clear that the view that represents Him as trying to spiritualize the eschatological Messianic expectations of His time cannot be sustained. In a series of passages He speaks in a quite realistic way of the coming of the Son of Man and the Messianic Kingdom when this world comes to an end. If one abandons the reinterpretation or rejects these passages, two alternatives remain: either to recognize and admit that Jesus really did live with a belief in the ideas of late Jewish eschatology or to assert that only those sayings are genuine in which He speaks in a truly spiritual way of the Messiah and the Messianic Kingdom. The remainder must then have been attributed to Him by a primitive Christianity that had reverted to the realistic views of late Judaism.

Faced by these alternatives, research at first decided for the second. That Jesus should be thought to have shared the Messianic ideas of late Judaism, which are so alien to our ideas, seemed so incomprehensible and so shocking that one preferred to doubt the trustworthiness of the two oldest Gospels and to deny the authenticity of a portion of the sayings they report.

But when this theory endeavors, as in the works of Timothy Colani (*Jésus Christ et les croyances messianiques de son temps*, 1864) and Gustave Volkmar (*Jesus Nazarenus*, 1882), to establish this distinction between genuine "spiritual Messianic" and spurious "eschatological Messianic" pronouncements, it must be denied that Jesus ever believed Himself to be the Messiah. For the passages in which He entrusts to His disciples the secret that He is the Messiah are, one and all, "eschatological Messianic," in that, according to them, He holds Himself to be the person who at the end of the world will appear as the Son of Man.

The question of whether Jesus thought eschatologically or not leads therefore to one point: Did He consider Himself to be the Messiah or not? Anyone who admits that He did must also admit that His ideas and expectations conformed to the eschatological views of late Judaism. Anyone who refuses to recognize this Jewish element in His thought must also refuse to attribute to Him any consciousness of being the Messiah.

That is the conclusion William Wrede drew in his work *The Messianic Secret of the Gospels* (1901). He developed the idea that Jesus presented Himself only as the Master and that after His death He became the Messiah in the imagination of His disciples. Only at a later stage of primitive Christianity was the idea introduced that Jesus did not reveal Himself as the Messiah but guarded it as a secret.

To doubt the eschatological Messianic statements of Jesus leads, then, with inexorable logic to the conclusion that there is nothing in the two oldest Gospels which can be accepted as historical beyond a few quite general reports about the teaching activities of a certain Jesus of Nazareth. Rather than become prey to such radicalism, scholarship resigned itself to the necessity of recognizing eschatological

Messianic ideas in Jesus' thought. Toward the end of the nineteenth century, the idea of the eschatological character of the message of Jesus and the thought that Jesus was aware of His role as Messiah gained increasing recognition. This view was especially well articulated by the Heidelberg theologian Johannes Weiss in his book *The Sermons of Jesus Concerning the Kingdom of God* (1892). Nevertheless, historical theology secretly hoped not to have to admit that Weiss could have been correct. In reality, however, theology had to go further. Weiss had gone only partway. He realized that Jesus thought eschatologically but did not conclude from this that His actions were also determined by eschatology. Weiss explained the course of Jesus' activity and His resolution to die using the hypothesis that He was initially successful and later a failure. For a historical understanding of the life of Jesus, however, it is necessary to consider that Jesus' actions cannot be explained through ordinary psychology, but solely on the basis of eschatological concepts.

I developed this eschatological solution to the problems of the life of Jesus in my work *The Quest of the Historical Jesus*. Earlier, in 1901, I had already sketched out these thoughts in *The Secret of Jesus' Messiahship and Passion*.

Because this eschatological solution succeeds in making the thoughts, words, and acts of Jesus consistent and comprehensible, it shows that many passages in the Gospels, which had been considered apocryphal in the past, were indeed intelligible and completely authentic.

In this way the eschatological interpretation of the life of Jesus puts an end to any need to doubt the credibility of the Gospels of Mark and Matthew. It shows that their accounts of the public activity and death of Jesus follow a faithful tradition that is reliable even in its details. If some elements of this tradition are obscure or confusing, the explanation lies chiefly in the fact that in a number of instances the disciples themselves did not understand the sayings and actions of their Master.

After the publication of my *Quest of the Historical Jesus* a friendly exchange of letters began between William Wrede and myself. It moved me deeply to learn from him that he suffered from an incurable heart disease and might expect death at any moment. "Subjectively I am tolerably well; objectively my condition is hopeless," he wrote in one of the last letters I received from him. The thought that I could work without thinking of my health while he had to give up his work in the best years of his life troubled me deeply. The tribute I had paid in my book to his achievements perhaps compensated a little for the hostility he had encountered in response to his courageous search for the truth. He died in 1907.

To my astonishment my work met at once with recognition in England. The first to make my views known there was Professor William Sanday of Oxford in his lectures on the problems of the life of Jesus. Unfortunately I could not accept his invitation to come to England because I had no time. I was studying medicine by then and just at that time, in addition to the preparation of my theological lectures, was at work on the German edition of my book on Bach, which had originally been written in French. Thus I missed a second opportunity to become acquainted with England.

In Cambridge Professor Francis Crawford Burkitt championed my work and secured its publication in English. The excellent translation was made by his pupil, the Reverend W. Montgomery. My exchanges with these two men soon led to a warm friendship.

While Professor Burkitt saw my views from a purely

scientific perspective, they met with Dr. Sanday's approval because they supported his own religious position. The modern image of Jesus as represented by the liberal school of Protestants did not agree with his Catholic leanings. I do not here criticize liberal Protestantism, to which I myself subscribe, but I disagree with some of its representatives, such as Colani and Wrede, already challenged by other liberals, for example Sabatier, Ménégoz, and Gognel.

My work also had significance for George Tyrrell. Without scientific documentation of the view that the thought and the actions of Jesus were conditioned by eschatology, he would not have been able, in his *Christianity at the Cross-Roads* (1910), to portray Jesus as the ethical Apocalyptic who by His very nature was not Protestant but Catholic.

The Historical Jesus and the Christianity of Today

6

As my two books on the life of Jesus gradually became known, the question was put to me from all sides: What can the eschatological Jesus, who lives expecting the end of the world and a supernatural Kingdom of God, be to us? I myself had always been preoccupied with this question during my studies for my books. The satisfaction, which I could not help feeling, of having solved so many historical riddles about the existence of Jesus was accompanied by the painful awareness that this new knowledge in the realm of history would mean unrest and difficulty for Christian piety. I comforted myself, however, with the words of St. Paul that had been familiar to me from childhood: "We can do nothing against the truth, but for the truth" (2 Corinthians 13:8).

Since the essential nature of the spiritual is truth, every new truth represents a gain. Truth is under all circumstances more valuable than nontruth, and this must apply to truth in the realm of history as well as to other kinds of truth. Even if it comes in a guise that piety finds strange and which at first creates difficulties, the final result can never be harmful. It can only mean a deeper piety. Religion has, therefore, nothing to fear from a confrontation with historical truth.

How strong would Christian truth stand in the world today if its relationship to truth in history were in every respect what it should be! Instead of acknowledging its rights, whenever historical truth was embarrassing, it was presented in some guise, consciously or unconsciously twisted, falsified, or denied. Today Christianity finds itself in a situation where pursuing historical truth freely is difficult because it has been neglected again and again in the past.

For example, we find ourselves in an awkward position because the early Christians published the writings of the Apostles without being sure of their authenticity. For generations this issue has been a source of sensitive debate. Some feel that, in view of the abundance of material, one cannot exclude the possibility that passages in the New Testament are not authentic in spite of the valuable content in them that we have learned to love. On the other side, there are those who want to save the reputation of early Christianity by stressing that this hypothesis cannot be proven. Yet those who were responsible for this debate were scarcely aware of doing anything wrong. They only followed the general custom of antiquity, which consisted in attributing to famous people works that in reality were not their own but expressed their ideas. Because I have studied the history of early Christianity and often had occasion to see the deficiencies concerning historical truth, I have become an ardent defender of the truth in our Christianity today.

Ideally, Jesus would have preached religious truth in a timeless way and in terms accessible to all succeeding generations. That, however, He did not do, and there is no doubt a reason for it.

We must therefore reconcile ourselves to the fact that Jesus' religion of love made its appearance as part of a system of thought that anticipated the imminent end of the world. We cannot make His images our own. We must transpose them into our modern concepts of the world. We have done this somewhat covertly until now.

In spite of what the words of the text said, we managed to interpret Jesus' teaching as if it were in agreement with our own worldview. Today, however, it is evident that we cannot adapt the teachings of Jesus to our modern concepts: we must find some method of interpretation legitimized by necessity. We must then recognize that religious truth can also pass through various stages.

How is this to be understood? So far as its essential spiritual and ethical nature is concerned, Christianity's religious truth remains the same through the centuries. There are only exterior changes caused by different worldviews.

Thus Jesus' religion of love, which made its first appearance within the framework of late Jewish eschatological expectation, continues in the late Greek, the medieval, and the modern views of the world. Throughout the centuries it remains the same. Whether it is interpreted in terms of one or another system of thought is of secondary importance. What is decisive is solely the influence that the spiritual and ethical truth of this religion has had on mankind from its beginning.

Unlike those who listened to the sermons of Jesus, we of today do not expect to see a Kingdom of God that realizes itself in supernatural events. We believe that it can only come into existence through the power of the spirit of Jesus working in our hearts and in the world. The one important thing is that we be as thoroughly dominated by the idea of the Kingdom of God as Jesus required His followers to be.

Jesus introduced into the late Jewish Messianic expectation the powerful idea, expressed in the Beatitudes of the Sermon on the Mount, that we may come to know God and belong to Him through love. Jesus is not concerned with spiritualizing realistic ideas of the Kingdom of God and of blessedness. But the spirituality that is the life of this religion of love purifies like a flame all ideas that come into contact with it. It is the destiny of Christianity to develop through a constant process of spiritualization.

Jesus never undertakes to expound the late Jewish dogmas of the Messiah and the Kingdom. His concern is not how believers see things, but that they be motivated by love, without which no one can belong to God and attain His Kingdom. The Messianic dogma remains in the background. If He did not happen to mention it now and then, one could forget that it is presupposed at all. That explains why it was possible for so long to overlook the fact that His religion of love was conditioned by the times in which He lived. The late Jewish view of the world, centered in the expectation of the Messiah, is the crater from which the flame of the eternal religion of love erupted.

The preacher does not have to expound again and again the meaning of this or that passage on the Messianic concept of the end of the world. To bring the message of Jesus to the men and women of our time, it suffices that they realize that Jesus Himself lived in expectation of the end of the world and of a Kingdom of God. But whoever preaches the Gospel of Jesus to them must explain for himself what His sayings originally meant, and must work his way through the historical truth to the eternal. During this process he will soon realize that the historical circumstances will open his eyes, that he will for the first time realize all that Jesus has to say to us.

Many theologians have confirmed my experience that the Jesus who is known historically, though He speaks to us from a world of thought other than our own, makes preaching not more difficult but easier. It is profoundly significant that whenever we hear the sayings of Jesus we have to enter a realm of thought that is not our own. Our own affirmative attitude toward the world and toward life constantly threatens to externalize Christianity.

The Gospel of Jesus that tells us to expect the end of the world turns us away from the path of immediate action toward service in behalf of the Kingdom of God. It urges us to seek true strength through detachment from this world in the spirit of the Kingdom of God. The essence of Christianity is an affirmation of the world that has passed through a negation of the world. Within a system of thought that denies the world and anticipates its end, Jesus sets up the eternal ethic of active love!

If the historical Jesus has something strange about Him, His personality as it really is still has a much stronger influence on us than the Jesus of dogma or critical scholarship. In dogma His personality loses its liveliness. Scholarship has so far modernized, and thus reduced, him.

Anyone who ventures to look the historical Jesus straight in the face and to listen for what He may have to teach him in His powerful sayings soon ceases to ask what this strange-seeming Jesus can still be to him. He learns to know Him as the One who claims authority over him.

The true understanding of Jesus is the understanding of will acting on will. The true relation to Him is to become His. Christian piety of any and every sort is valuable only insofar as it means the surrender of our will to His.

Today Jesus does not require men to be able to grasp either in word or in thought who He is. He did not think it necessary to give those who actually heard His sayings any insight into the secret of His personality, or to disclose to them the fact that He was that descendant of David who was one day to be revealed as the Messiah. The one thing He did require of them was that in both thought and deed they should prove themselves men who had been compelled by Him to rise from being of this world to being other than the world, and thereby partakers of His peace.

As I studied and thought about Jesus, all this became certain in my mind. Because of this, I concluded my *Quest of the Historical Jesus* with these words: "As one unknown and nameless He comes to us, just as on the shore of the lake He approached those men who knew him not. His words are the same: 'Follow thou Me!' and He puts us to the tasks He has to carry out in our age. He commands. And to those who obey, be they wise or simple, He will reveal Himself in the fellowship of peace and activity, of struggle and suffering, till they come to know, as an inexpressible secret, Who He is . . ."

Many people are shocked upon learning that the historical Jesus must be accepted as "capable of error" because the supernatural Kingdom of God, the manifestation of which He announced as imminent, did not appear. What can we do in the face of what stands clearly recorded in the Gospels?

Are we acting in the spirit of Jesus if we attempt with hazardous and sophisticated explanations to force the sayings into agreement with the dogmatic teaching of His absolute and universal infallibility? He Himself never made any claim to such omniscience. Just as He pointed out to the young man who addressed Him as "Good Master" (Mark 10:17ff.) that God alone is good, so He would also have set Himself against those who would have liked to attribute to Him a divine infallibility. Knowledge of spiritual truth cannot be proved by displaying further knowledge about the events of world history and matters of ordinary life. Its province lies on a different plane from the knowledge of the affairs of this world, and it is quite independent of it.

Jesus no doubt fits His teaching into the late Jewish Messianic dogma. But He does not think dogmatically. He formulates no doctrine. Nowhere does He demand of His hearers that they sacrifice thinking to believing. Quite the contrary! He bids them to reflect upon religion. Within the Messianic hopes His hearers carry in their hearts, He kindles the fire of an ethical faith. The truth that the ethical is the essence of religion is firmly established on the authority of Jesus.

Beyond this, the religion of love taught by Jesus has been freed from any dogmatism that clung to it with the disappearance of the late Jewish expectation of the immediate end of the world. The mold in which the casting was made has been broken. We are now at liberty to let the religion of Jesus become a living force in our thought, as its purely spiritual and ethical nature demands. We recognize the deep values of Christianity as transmitted by early Greek teaching and kept alive by the piety of many centuries. We hold fast to the Church with love, reverence, and gratitude. But we belong to her as men who appeal to the saying of the Apostle Paul, "Where the Spirit of the Lord is, there is liberty," and who believe that they serve Christianity better by the strength of their devotion to Jesus' religion of love than by submission to all the articles of faith. If the Church abides by the spirit of Jesus, there is room in her for every form of Christian piety, even for that which claims unrestricted freedom.

I find it no easy task to pursue my vocation, to admonish Christian faith to come to terms with itself in all sincerity with historical truth. But I have devoted myself to it with joy, because I am certain that truthfulness in all things belongs to the spirit of Jesus.

My Work on Bach

7

While I was working on *The Quest of the Historical Jesus* I finished a book in French on J. S. Bach. Widor, with whom I used to spend several weeks in Paris every spring, and frequently also in the autumn, had complained that only biographical works were available about Bach in French, and nothing that would introduce people to his art. I had to promise him that I would spend the autumn vacation of 1902 writing an essay on the nature of Bach's art for the students of the Paris Conservatory.

This task appealed to me because it

gave me an opportunity to express thoughts at which I had arrived in the course of my theoretical and practical study of Bach, as organist to the Bach Society at St. Wilhelm's. This society was founded in 1887 by Ernest Münch, the organist of the Church of St. Wilhelm, with whom I had many discussions on the interpretation of Bach. I owe him much. Charles Münch, the distinguished conductor, was his son.

At the end of the vacation, in spite of the most strenuous work, I had gotten no further than preliminary studies for the treatise. It had also become clear that this would expand into a book on Bach. With good courage I resigned myself to my fate.

In 1903 and 1904 I devoted all my spare time to Bach. My work was eased by my having acquired a complete edition of his works, which was at that time rarely available and then only at a very high price. I was thus no longer forced to study the scores in the university library, a restriction which had been a great hindrance, since I could hardly find any time for Bach except at night. I happened to learn at a music shop in Strasbourg of a lady in Paris who, in order to support the enterprise of the Bach Society, had been a subscriber to the complete edition. She now wanted to get rid of the long row of big gray volumes that took up so much space on her bookshelves. Pleased at being able to give somebody pleasure with them, she let me have them for the ridiculously small sum of two hundred marks (one hundred dollars). This stroke of luck seemed to be a good omen for the success of my work.

It was, in truth, a very rash undertaking on my part to start writing a book on Bach. Although, thanks to extensive reading, I had some knowledge of music history and theory,

I had not studied music as one studies for a profession. However, my intention was not to produce new historical material about Bach and his time. As a musician I wanted to talk to other musicians about Bach's music. So I resolved that the main subject of my work should be what in most books hitherto had been too slightly treated, namely the real nature of Bach's music and its interpretation. Biographical and historical aspects are only given as an introduction.

If the difficulties in treating such a subject made me fear that I had embarked on a task beyond my powers, I consoled myself with the thought that I was not writing for Germany, the home of Bach scholarship, but for France, where the art of the Cantor of St. Thomas was yet to be made known.

To write the book in French at a time when I was also lecturing and preaching in German was an effort. It is true that ever since my childhood I have spoken French as readily as German. I always used French in my letters to my parents because that was the custom in my family. German, however, is my mother tongue, because the Alsatian dialect, which is my native language, is Germanic.

I profited much in my work on Bach by the stylistic criticism of my manuscript by Hubert Gillot, at that time a lecturer in French at the University of Strasbourg. He impressed upon me the fact that the French sentence needs rhythm in far stronger measure than does the German. I can best describe the difference between the two languages by saying that in French I seem to be strolling along the well-kept paths of a fine park, but in German to be wandering at will in a magnificent forest. Into literary German new life continually flows from the dialects with which it has kept in touch. French has lost this ever fresh contact with the soil. It is rooted in its literature, and has thereby become, in the positive as well as the pejorative sense of the word, something finished, while German in the same way remains something unfinished. The perfection of French consists in its being able to express a thought in the clearest and most concise way; that of German in being able to present it in its manifold aspects. I consider Rousseau's *Social Contract* to be the greatest linguistic creation in French. In German, in my view, Luther's translation of the Bible and Nietzsche's *Jenseits von Gut und Böse* (*Beyond Good and Evil*) come closest to perfection. Always accustomed in French to be careful about the rhythmical arrangement of the sentence and to strive for simplicity of expression, I required the same in German as well. And now through my work on the French *Bach* it became clear to me what literary style corresponded to my nature.

Like everyone who writes about art, I had to wrestle with the difficulty of expressing artistic opinions and impressions in words. When we speak about art, we can speak only in approximations, in parables.

In the autumn of 1904 I was able to announce to Widor, who had spurred me on again and again with letters and who was now in Venice, where he was spending his holiday, that the undertaking was at last completed. He immediately wrote the preface, which he had promised me.

The book appeared in 1905, dedicated to Mme Mathilde Schweitzer, the wife of my father's eldest brother in Paris. Had she not enabled me to meet Widor in 1893 and, thanks to her hospitable house, given me again and again the opportunity of being with him, I should never have come to be writing about Bach.

I was surprised and delighted that my work met with recognition even in Germany as a valuable contribution to the study of Bach, though I had written it merely to fill a gap in French musical literature. In the journal *Kunstwart* (*Art Guardian*) von Lüpke suggested a translation. Consequently, in the autumn of that year, 1905, a German edition was agreed upon, to be published by Breitkopf und Härtel.

When in the summer of 1906, after the completion of *The Quest of the Historical Jesus*, I turned to work on the German edition of *Bach*, I soon realized that it was impossible for me to translate it into another language myself, and that in order to write anything satisfactory, I had to plunge anew into the original materials of my book. So I closed the French *Bach* and resolved to make a new and better German one. Out of a book of 455 pages there emerged, to the dismay of the astonished publisher, one of 844. The first pages of the new work I wrote at Bayreuth in the Black Horse Inn after a wonderful performance of *Tristan*. For weeks I had been trying in vain to get to work. In the mood of exaltation in which I returned from the Festival Hill, I succeeded. Accompanied by the babble of voices from the Bierhalle below, I began to write, and it was long after sunrise before I laid down my pen. From that time onward I felt such joy in the work that I concluded it in two years, although my medical courses, the preparation of my lectures, my preaching activities, and my concert tours prevented me from working on the manuscript as much as I would have liked. I frequently had to put it aside for weeks at a time.

The German edition appeared early in 1908. It is from this text that Ernest Newman made his splendid translation into English.

In their fight against Wagner, the anti-Wagnerites appealed
to the ideal of classical music as they saw it. For them, this
"pure music" excluded any poetic or descriptive elements,
and its only intention was to create beautiful harmonies to
absolute perfection. They cited the example of Bach, whose
works had become better known in the second half of the
nineteenth century, thanks to the edition of the Bach Society at Leipzig. They also claimed Mozart, and they op-
posed Wagner. Bach's fugues especially seemed to them
the indisputable proof that he served their ideal of pure
music. He was depicted as a classic of this kind by Philipp
Spitta in his important, comprehensive work, the first in
which biographical material was based on careful examination of sources (1873–1880).

As a contrast to the Bach of pure music I present the
Bach who is a poet and painter in sound. In his music and
in his texts he expresses the emotional as well as the descriptive with great vitality and clarity. Before all else he
aims at rendering the pictorial in lines of sound. He is even
more tone painter than tone poet. His art is nearer to that
of Berlioz than to that of Wagner. If the text speaks of
drifting mists, of boisterous winds, of roaring rivers, of
waves that ebb and flow, of leaves falling from the tree,
of bells that toll for the dying, of the confident faith that
walks with firm steps or the weak faith that falters, of the
proud who will be debased and the humble who will be
exalted, of Satan rising in rebellion, of angels on the
clouds of heaven, then one sees and hears all this in his
music.

Bach has, in fact, his own language of sound. There are
in his music constantly recurring rhythmical motives expressing peaceful bliss, lively joy, intense pain, or sorrow
sublimely borne.

The impulse to express poetic and pictorial concepts is
the essence of music. It addresses itself to the listener's
creative imagination and seeks to kindle in him the feelings
and visions with which the music was composed. But this

it can do only if the person who uses the language of sound possesses the mysterious faculty of rendering thoughts with a superior clarity and precision. In this respect Bach is the greatest of the great.

His music is poetic and descriptive because its themes are born of poetic and pictorial ideas. Out of these themes the composition unfolds, a finished piece of architecture in lines of sound. What is in its essence poetic and pictorial music appears as Gothic architecture transformed into sound. What is greatest in this art, so full of natural life, so wonderfully plastic, and unique in the perfection of its form, is the spirit that emanates from it. A soul that longs for peace out of the world's unrest and has itself already tasted peace allows others to share its experience in this music.

In order to produce its full effect, the art of Bach must be performed with lively and perfect plasticity. This principle, which is fundamental to its interpretation, is not always recognized.

To begin with, it is a crime against the style of Bach's music that we perform it with huge orchestras and enormous choirs. The cantatas and the Passion music were written for choirs of twenty-five to thirty voices and an orchestra of about the same number. Bach's orchestra does not accompany the choir: it is a partner with equal rights. There is no such thing as an orchestral equivalent to a choir of a hundred and fifty voices. We therefore should provide for the performance of Bach's music choirs of forty to fifty voices and orchestras of fifty to sixty instrumentalists. The wonderful interweaving of the voice parts must stand out, clear and distinct. For alto and soprano, Bach did not use women's voices but boys' voices only, even for the solos. Choirs of male voices form a homogeneous whole. At the very least, then, women's voices should be supplemented with boys', but the ideal is that even the alto and soprano solos be sung by boys.

Since the music of Bach is architectural, the crescendos

and decrescendos, which in Beethoven's and post-Bee-thoven music are responses to emotional experiences, are not appropriate. Alternations of forte and piano are significant only insofar as they serve to emphasize leading phrases and to leave subsidiary ones less prominent. It is only within the limits of these alternations of forte and piano that declamatory crescendos and diminuendos are admissible. If they obliterate the difference between forte and piano, they ruin the architecture of the composition.

Since a Bach fugue always begins and ends with a main theme, it cannot tolerate any beginning and ending in piano.

Bach is played altogether too fast. Music that presupposes a visual comprehension of lines of sound advancing side by side becomes chaos for the listener; high speed makes comprehension impossible.

Yet it is not so much by tempo as by phrasing—which makes the lines of sound stand out before the listener in a living plasticity—that appreciation for the life that animates Bach's music is made possible.

Down to the middle of the nineteenth century, Bach was generally played, curiously enough, staccato, but players since then have gone to the other extreme of rendering him with a monotonous legato. But as time went on, it occurred to me that Bach calls for phrasing that is full of life. He thinks as a violinist. His notes should be connected and at the same time separated from one another in a way that is natural to the bowing of a violin. To play one of Bach's piano compositions well means to play it as it would be performed by a string quartet.

Correct phrasing is to be attained by correct accenting. Bach demands that the notes decisive in the musical design are given an accent. A characteristic of each section's structure is that as a rule they do not start with an accent but strive to reach one. They are conceived as beginning with an upward beat. In addition, in Bach the accents of the lines of sound do not as a rule coincide with the natural accents of the bars but advance side by side with them in their own way. From this tension between the accents of the line of sound and those of the bars comes the extraordinary rhythmical vitality of Bach's music.

These are the external requirements for the performance of Bach's music. Above and beyond those, his music demands that we men and women attain the composure and inwardness that will enable us to bring to life something of the deep spirit lying hidden within it.

The ideas I put forward about the nature of Bach's music and the appropriate way of rendering it found recognition because they appeared just at the right time. The interest aroused by the publication toward the end of the last century of the complete edition of his works had made the musical world aware that Bach was not synonymous with academic and classical music. People were also in the dark about the traditional method of performing it, and they began to look for a method that would match Bach's style. But this new knowledge had as yet neither been formulated nor grounded. And so my book aired for the first time the views that musicians especially concerned with Bach had been mulling over in their minds. Thus I won many a friend.

With pleasure I think of the many delightful letters it brought me immediately after it appeared. Felix Mottl, the conductor, whom I had admired from a distance, wrote to me from Leipzig, after having read the book straight through without a break, in the train and in his hotel on his way to that town from Munich, where some friends had given him the book for the journey. I met him soon after, and later on several occasions enjoyed some happy hours with him.

It was through this book that I became acquainted with Siegfried Ochs, the Berlin Bach conductor, and developed a friendship that has grown continually closer.

Carmen Sylva, Queen of Romania, wrote me a long letter because I had made her beloved Bach still dearer to her, and it was followed by a whole series of others. The latest of them, directed to Africa, was painfully written with a pencil because her hand, which suffered from rheumatism, could no longer hold a pen. I could not accept the frequently repeated invitation of this regal friend to spend my vacation at her castle in Sinaya, which carried with it the obligation to play the organ for her two hours a day. In the last years before my departure for Africa I could not afford the time for a holiday. By the time I did return home she was no longer among the living.

On Organs and
Organ Building

8

As a corollary to the book on Bach, I published a study on the construction of organs. I had written it in the fall of 1905, before beginning my medical studies.

From my grandfather Schillinger I had inherited an interest in organ building, which impelled me, while still a boy, to get to know all about the workings of an organ.

The organs of the late nineteenth century had a strange effect on me. Although they were praised as miracles of advanced technology, I could find no pleasure in them. In the au-

tumn of 1896, after my first visit to Bayreuth, I made a
detour to Stuttgart. There I examined the new organ in the
Liederhalle of that town, about which the newspapers had
published enthusiastic reports. Herr Lang, the organist of
the Stiftskirche, an outstanding musician and personality,
was kind enough to show it to me. When I heard the harsh
tone of the much praised instrument, and when in the Bach
fugue Lang played for me I perceived a chaos of sounds in
which I could not distinguish the separate voices, my suspicion that the modern organ was a step not forward but
backward suddenly became a certainty.

To confirm my suspicion and to find out why this should
be so, I used my free time over the next few years getting
to know as many organs, old and new, as possible. I also
talked with all the organists and organ builders with whom
I came in contact. As a rule I met with ridicule and jeers.
The pamphlet in which I undertook to define the qualities
of the true organ was also understood at first by only a
scattered few. It appeared in 1906, ten years after my visit
to Stuttgart, and bears the title *The Art of Organ-Building
and Organ-Playing in Germany and France.* In it I acknowledge a preference for the French style of organ building over the German, because in several respects it has
remained faithful to the traditions of the art.

If the old organs sound better than those built today, it is
often because they have been better positioned. The best
place for an organ, if the nave of the church is not too long,
is above the entrance, opposite the chancel. There it stands
high and free, and the sound can travel unhindered in every
direction.

In the case of very long naves it is better to build the

organ at a certain height on the side wall of the nave, about
halfway along it, thereby avoiding the echo that would spoil
the clarity of the playing. There are still many European
cathedrals in which the organ hangs thus, like a "swallow's
nest," for example in the Cathedral at Strasbourg, pro-
jecting into the middle of the nave. Placed like this, an
organ of forty stops develops the power of one with sixty!

Today the effort to build organs as large as possible combined with the object of having the organ and the choir
close together frequently places the organ in an unfavorable
position.

If there is room in the gallery above the entrance only
for a moderate-sized organ, as is often the case, the instrument is placed in the chancel, an arrangement that has the
practical advantage of keeping the organ and the choir close
together. But an organ standing on the ground can never
produce the same sound effect as one placed above. From
the ground position the sound is hindered in its expansion,
especially if the church is full. How many organs, particularly in England, while good in themselves, are unable to
produce their full effect because of their position in the
chancel!

The alternative method of positioning organ and choir
close together is to devote the western gallery to the choir
and the orchestra (if there is one) and to place the organ
in some confined and vaulted space where it cannot sound
properly. Among some modern architects it is assumed that
any corner will do for the organ.

In recent times architects and organ builders have begun
to overcome the difficulty of distance, thanks to pneumatic
or electric connections between keyboard and pipes. The
different parts of the organ can now be put in different
places and still sound together. This technique has become
especially common in America, and the effects may impress
the crowd. The organ can only display its full, majestic
effects however, as a unified instrument. Then, from its

natural place above the listeners, the sounds can flood the nave of the church.

If the church is good-sized and has a strong chorus and orchestra, the only correct solution to the choir and organ problem is to place both chorus and orchestra in the church's choir, with a small organ standing near them for accompaniment. If that is done it is of course impossible for the organist at the large organ to be at the same time the conductor of the chorus.

The best organs were built between about 1850 and 1880, when organ builders, who were artists, availed themselves of technological developments in order to realize as completely as they could the ideals of Silbermann and the other great organ builders of the eighteenth century. The most important of them is Aristide Cavaillé-Col, the creator of the organs at St. Sulpice and Notre Dame in Paris. The organ in St. Sulpice—completed in 1862—I consider to be, in spite of a few deficiencies, the finest of all the organs I know. It functions as well today as it did on the first day, and with proper maintenance it will do the same two centuries hence. The organ in Notre Dame has suffered from being exposed to the inclemencies of weather during the war, when the stained-glass windows were removed. Many a time have I met the venerable Cavaillé-Col—he died in 1899—at the organ in St. Sulpice, where he used to appear for the service every Sunday. One of his favorite maxims was: "An organ sounds best when there is so much space between the pipes that a man can get round each one."

Of the other representative organ builders of that period I value especially Ladegast in northern Germany, Walcker in southern Germany, and certain English and northern masters who, like Ladegast, were influenced by Cavaillé-Col.

Toward the end of the nineteenth century the master organ builders became organ manufacturers, and those who were not willing to follow this course were ruined. Since that time people no longer ask whether an organ has a good tone, but ask whether it is provided with every possible modern arrangement for altering the stops, and whether it contains the greatest possible number of stops for the lowest possible price. With incredible blindness they tear out the beautiful old works of their organs; instead of restoring them with reverence and the care they deserve, they replace them with products of the factory.

Holland is the country with the greatest appreciation for the beauty and value of old organs. The organists of that country were not discouraged by the difficulties of playing the old instruments with some of their technical disadvantages. As a result there are in the churches of Holland today numerous organs, large and small, which with appropriate restoration will in the course of time lose their technical imperfections and keep their beauty of sound. There is scarcely any country so rich as Holland in splendid old organ cases as well.

Little by little the idea of reform in organ building that I had put forward in my essay began to attract attention. At the Congress of the International Music Society held in Vienna in 1909, on the suggestion of Guido Adler, provision was made for the first time for a section on organ building. In this section some like-minded members joined me in working out a set of "International Regulations for Organ Building," which put an end to the blind admiration for purely technical achievements and called for the production once more of carefully built instruments of fine tone.

In the years that followed people perceived that the really good organ must combine the beautiful tone of the old organs with the technical advantages of the new. Twenty-two years after its first appearance, my essay on organ building was reprinted without change as the generally accepted program of reform; with an appendix on the present state of the organ-building industry it thus became a kind of jubilee edition.

Although the monumental organs of the eighteenth century, as they were later perfected by Cavaillé-Col and others, are to my mind the ideal so far as tone is concerned, lately in Germany historians of music have been trying to return to the organ of Bach's day. That, however, is not the ideal organ, only its forerunner. It lacks the majestic sonority that is part of the organ's essential nature. Art aims at the absolute; it does not establish the archaic as its ideal. We may say of it, "When that which is perfect has come, that which is incomplete shall disappear."

Although these simple truths about how to produce an artistically sound organ have by now been recognized, their practical application is overdue. That is because organs are built today in factories on a large scale. Commercial interests obstruct artistic ones. The carefully built and really effective organ ends up being 30 percent more expensive than the factory organ, which dominates the market. The organ builder who wants to supply something really good, therefore, risks his all on the venture. Very rarely indeed can church authorities be persuaded that they are right in paying for an instrument with thirty-three stops a sum that could procure them one with forty.

I was talking once at Strasbourg about organs and organ

building to a confectioner with musical tastes, and he said to me, "So it's just the same with organ building as with confectionery! People today don't know what a good organ is, nor do they know what good confectionery is. No one remembers how things taste that are made with fresh milk, fresh cream, fresh butter, fresh eggs, the best oil, and the best lard, and natural fruit juice, and are sweetened with sugar and nothing else. They are, one and all, accustomed nowadays to find quite satisfactory what is made with canned milk, dehydrated egg, with the cheapest oil and the cheapest lard, with synthetic fruit juice and any sort of sweetening, because they are not offered anything different. Not understanding what quality means, they are satisfied so long as things look nice. If I were to attempt to make and sell the good things I used to make, I would lose my customers, because, like the good organ builder, I would be about thirty percent too expensive. . . ."

Through my organ recitals in almost all the countries of Europe I realize how far we still are from the ideal instrument. Yet the day must come when organists will demand really sound, well-built instruments, and will force organ builders to abandon the production of factory organs. But when will the ideal triumph over circumstance?

I have sacrificed a great deal of time and labor to struggle for the true organ. I have spent many a night over organ designs sent to me for approval or revision. I have undertaken many journeys to study on the spot the problems involved in restoring or rebuilding an organ. I have written hundreds of letters to bishops, deans, presidents of consistories, mayors, ministers, church committees, church elders, organ builders, and organists, trying to convince them that they ought to restore their fine old organs instead of replacing them with new ones; and I have urged them to consider the quality, not the number, of the stops, and to spend money to have pipes made of the best material, and not to equip the console with superfluous alterations in the registers. And how often did these many letters, these many journeys, and these many conversations prove ultimately futile, because the people concerned decided finally for the factory organ, the specifications for which look so fine on paper!

The hardest struggles went to preserving the old organs. What eloquence I had to employ to obtain the rescinding of death sentences that had already been passed on beautiful old organs! How many organists received the news with the same incredulous laughter—as did Sarah when she received the news that she was to have descendants!—that the organs they prized so little, because of their age and their ruinous condition, were beautiful instruments and must be preserved. How many organists were changed from friends to foes because I was the obstacle to their plan of replacing their old organ with one built in a factory! I was also taken to task for my advice that they accept fewer registers than they had proposed for the sake of quality.

Today I still have to look on helplessly while noble old organs are rebuilt and enlarged until not a trace of their original beauty is left, just because they are not powerful enough to suit present-day taste. Occasionally I still even see them dismantled and replaced at great cost by vulgar products of the factory!

The first old organ I rescued—and what a task it was!—was Silbermann's fine instrument at St. Thomas, Strasbourg.

"In Africa he saves old blacks, in Europe old organs" is what my friends said of me.

The building of the so-called giant organs I consider to be a modern aberration. An organ should be only as large as the nave of the church requires and the place reserved for it permits. A really good organ with seventy to eighty stops, if it stands at a certain height and has open space all round it, can fill the largest church. When asked to name the largest and finest organ in the world, I generally answer that from what I have heard and read there must be 127 that are the largest, and 137 that are the finest in the world.

I was not as interested in concert organs as I was in church organs. The best organs cannot sound with full effect in a concert hall. Owing to the crowds that fill the halls, the organ loses brilliance and fullness of tone. Moreover, architects generally push the concert organ into any corner that is convenient and where it cannot sound properly under any circumstances. The organ demands a stone-vaulted building in which the presence of a congregation does not mean that the room feels choked. In a concert hall an organ does not have the character of a solo instrument that it has in a church; rather, it accompanies or supplements choir and orchestra. Composers will certainly use an organ with the orchestra much more in the future than they have done in the past. Used in that way the resulting sound draws brilliance and flexibility from the orchestra and fullness from the organ. The technical significance of supplementing the modern orchestra with an organ is that the orchestra secures flutelike tones for its bass, and thus for the first time has a bass that corresponds in character to its higher notes.

Playing an organ with an orchestra in a concert hall gives me great joy. But if I find myself in the position of having to play it in such a hall as a solo instrument, I try not to treat it as a secular concert instrument. Through my choice of pieces and the way I play them, I try to turn the concert hall into a church. But best of all I like in both church and concert hall to introduce a choir and thus change the concert into a kind of service, in which the choir responds to the choral prelude of the organ by singing the chorale itself.

Because of the continuity of its tone, which can be maintained as long as desired, the organ has in it an element of the eternal. Even in a secular room it cannot become a secular instrument.

That I have had the joy of seeing my ideal of a church organ very largely realized in certain modern organs I owe to the artistic ability of the Alsatian organ builder Frédéric Haerpfer—who formed his ideas from the organs built by Silbermann—coupled with the good sense of those church councils that allowed themselves to be persuaded to order not the largest but the best organ that the money at their disposal could buy.

The work and the worry caused by my practical interest in organ building made me wish sometimes that I had never gotten involved in it. If I do not give it up, it is because the fight for a good organ is to my mind part of the fight for truth. And when on Sundays I think of this or that church in which a noble organ is ringing out because I saved it from being replaced by an unworthy instrument, I feel richly rewarded for all the time and trouble I have taken over the course of more than thirty years in the interests of organ building.

I Resolve to Become
a Jungle Doctor

9

On October 13, 1905, I dropped into a letter box on the avenue de la Grande Armée in Paris letters to my parents and to some of my closest friends telling them that at the beginning of the winter term I would embark on the study of medicine with the idea of later going out to equatorial Africa as a doctor. In one letter I submitted my resignation from the post of principal of the Collegium Wilhelmitanum (the theological seminary of St. Thomas) because of the time my studies would require.

The plan I hoped to realize had been

in my mind for some time. Long ago in my student days I had thought about it. It struck me as inconceivable that I should be allowed to lead such a happy life while I saw so many people around me struggling with sorrow and suffering. Even at school I had felt stirred whenever I caught a glimpse of the miserable home surroundings of some of my classmates and compared them with the ideal conditions in which we children of the parsonage at Günsbach had lived. At the university, enjoying the good fortune of studying and even getting some results in scholarship and the arts, I could not help but think continually of others who were denied that good fortune by their material circumstances or their health.

One brilliant summer morning at Günsbach, during the Whitsuntide holidays—it was in 1896—as I awoke, the thought came to me that I must not accept this good fortune as a matter of course, but must give something in return.

While outside the birds sang I reflected on this thought, and before I had gotten up I came to the conclusion that until I was thirty I could consider myself justified in devoting myself to scholarship and the arts, but after that I would devote myself directly to serving humanity. I had already tried many times to find the meaning that lay hidden in the saying of Jesus: "Whosoever would save his life shall lose it, and whosoever shall lose his life for My sake and the Gospels shall save it." Now I had found the answer. I could now add outward to inward happiness.

What the character of my future activities would be was not yet clear to me. I left it to chance to guide me. Only one thing was certain, that it must be direct human service, however inconspicuous its sphere.

I naturally thought first of some activity in Europe. I formed a plan for taking charge of and educating abandoned or neglected children, then making them pledge to help children later on in a similar situation in the same way. When in 1903, as director of the theological seminary I moved into my roomy and sunny official quarters on the second floor of the College of St. Thomas, I was in a position to begin the experiment. I offered help now in one place, now in another, but always to no avail. The charters of the organizations that looked after destitute and abandoned children had made no provisions for accepting volunteers. For example, when the Strasbourg orphanage burned down, I offered to take in a few boys temporarily, but the superintendent did not even let me finish my sentence. I made similar attempts elsewhere also in vain.

For a time I thought I would someday devote myself to tramps and discharged convicts. To prepare myself for this I joined the Reverend Augustus Ernst at St. Thomas in an undertaking he had begun. Between one and two in the afternoon he remained at home ready to speak to anyone who came to him asking for help or a night's lodging. He did not, however, give the applicant money, nor did he make him wait until the information about his circumstances could be confirmed. Instead he would offer to look up the applicant in his home or shelter that very afternoon and verify the information he had been given about the situation. After this, he would give him all necessary assistance for as long as was needed. How many bicycle rides did we make into town or the suburbs, and quite often only to find that the applicant was unknown at the address he had given. In many cases, however, it provided an opportunity for giving appropriate help, with knowledge of the circumstances. I also had friends who kindly contributed money to this cause.

As a student, I had been active in social service as a

member of the student association known as the Diaconate of St. Thomas, which held its meetings in the St. Thomas seminary. Each of us had a certain number of poor families assigned to him, which he was to visit every week, taking some aid and then reporting about their situation. The funds we thus distributed we collected from members of the old Strasbourg families who supported this undertaking, begun by earlier generations and now carried on by ourselves. Twice a year, if I remember correctly, each of us had to make a fixed number of financial appeals. For me, being shy and rather awkward in society, these visits were a torture. I believe that in this preparatory experience of soliciting funds, which I had to do much more of in later years, I sometimes showed myself extremely unskillful. However, I learned through them that soliciting with tact and restraint is better appreciated than any sort of aggressive approach, and also that correct soliciting methods include the friendly acceptance of refusal.

In our youthful inexperience we no doubt often failed, in spite of our best intentions, to use the money entrusted to us in the wisest way. The expectations of the givers were, however, fulfilled with respect to their purpose—that young men should devote themselves to serve the poor. For that reason I think with deep gratitude of those who met our efforts with so much understanding and generosity, and hope that many students may have the privilege of working as recruits in the struggle against poverty.

As I worried about the homeless and former convicts it became clear to me that they could only be effectively helped if many individuals devoted themselves to them. At the same time, however, I realized that in many cases individuals could only accomplish their tasks in collaboration with official organizations. But what I wanted was an absolutely personal and independent activity.

Although I was resolved to put my services at the disposal of some organization if it should become really necessary, I nonetheless never gave up the hope of finding an activity to which I could devote myself as an individual and as a wholly free agent. I have always considered it an ever renewed grace that I could fulfill this profound desire.

One morning in the autumn of 1904 I found on my writing table in the seminary one of the green-covered magazines in which the Paris Missionary Society (La Société Evangélique des Missions à Paris) reported on its activities every month. A Miss Scherdlin used to pass them on to me. She knew that in my youth I had been impressed by the letters from Mr. Casalis, one of the first missionaries of this society. My father had read them to us in his mission services.

Without paying much attention, I leafed through the magazine that had been put on my table the night before. As I was about to turn to my studies, I noticed an article with the headline "Les besoins de la Mission du Congo" ("The needs of the Congo Mission," in the *Journal des Missions Evangéliques*, June 1904). It was by Alfred Boegner, the president of the Paris Missionary Society, an Alsatian, who complained in it that the mission did not have enough people to carry on its work in the Gaboon, the northern province of the Congo colony. The writer expressed the hope that his appeal would bring some of those "on whom the Master's eyes already rested" to a decision to offer themselves for this urgent work. The article concluded: "Men and women who can reply simply to the Master's call, 'Lord, I am coming,' those are the people the Church needs." I finished my article and quietly began my work. My search was over.

I spent my thirtieth birthday a few months later like the man in the parable who, "desiring to build a tower, first calculates the cost of completion whether he has the means to complete it." The result was a resolve to realize my plan of direct human service in equatorial Africa.

Aside from one trustworthy friend, no one knew of my intention. When it became known through the letters I had sent from Paris, I had hard battles to fight with my relatives and friends. They reproached me more for not taking them into my confidence and discussing the decision with them than they did for the enterprise itself. With this secondary issue they tormented me beyond measure during those difficult weeks. That theological friends should outdo the others in their protests struck me as all the more absurd because they had no doubt all preached a fine sermon— perhaps a very fine one—that quoted Paul's declaration in his letter to the Galatians that he "did not confer with flesh or blood" before he knew what he would do for Jesus.

My relatives and friends reproached me for the folly of my enterprise. They said I was a man who was burying the talent entrusted to him and wanted to trade in false currency. I ought to leave work among Africans to those who would not thereby abandon gifts and achievements in scholarship and the arts. Widor, who loved me as a son, scolded me for acting like a general who, rifle in hand, insists on fighting in the firing line (there was no talk about trenches at that time). A lady who was filled with the modern spirit proved to me that I could do much more by lecturing on behalf of medical help for Africans than I could by the course of action I contemplated. The aphorism from Goethe's *Faust*, "In the beginning was the Deed," was now out of date, she said, "Today propaganda is the mother of events."

In the many adversarial debates I had to endure with people who passed for Christians, it amazed me to see them unable to perceive that the desire to serve the love preached by Jesus may sweep a man into a new course of life. They read in the New Testament that it can do so, and found it quite in order there.

I had assumed that familiarity with the sayings of Jesus would give a much better comprehension of what to popular logic is not rational. Several times, indeed, my appeal to the obedience that Jesus' command of love requires under certain circumstances earned me an accusation of conceit. How I suffered to see so many people assuming the right to tear open the doors and shutters of my inner self!

In general, neither allowing them to see that I was hurt nor letting them know the thought that had given birth to my resolution was of any use. They thought there must be something behind it all, and guessed at disappointment with the slow development of my career. For this there were no grounds at all, in that, even as a young man, I had received as much recognition as others usually get only after a whole life of toil and struggle. Unhappy love was another reason alleged for my decision.

The attitude of people who did not try to explore my feelings, but regarded me as a young man not quite right in the head and treated me with correspondingly affectionate ridicule, represented a real kindness.

I felt it to be quite natural in itself that family and friends should challenge the rationality of my plan. As one who demands that idealists should be sober in their views, I was aware that every venture down an untrodden path is a venture that looks sensible and likely to be successful only under unusual circumstances. In my own case I held the venture to be justified, because I had considered it for a long time and from every point of view, and I thought that I had good health, sound nerves, energy, practical common sense, toughness, prudence, very few wants, and everything else that might be necessary for the pursuit of my idea. I believed, further, that I had the inner fortitude to endure any eventual failure of my plan.

As a man of independent action, I have since that time been approached for my opinion and advice by many people who wanted to risk a similar venture. Only in comparatively few cases have I taken the responsibility of giving them encouragement. I often had to recognize that the need "to do something special" was born of a restless spirit. Such people wanted to dedicate themselves to larger tasks because those that lay nearest did not satisfy them. Often, too, it was evident that they were motivated by quite secondary considerations. Only a person who finds value in any kind of activity and who gives of himself with a full sense of service has the right to choose an exceptional task instead of following a common path. Only a person who feels his preference to be a matter of course, not something out of the ordinary, and who has no thought of heroism but only of a duty undertaken with sober enthusiasm, is capable of becoming the sort of spiritual pioneer the world needs. There are no heroes of action—only heroes of renunciation and suffering. Of these there are plenty. But few of them are known, and even they not to the crowd, but to the few.

Carlyle's *On Heroes and Hero-Worship* is not a profound book.

The majority of those who feel the impulse and are actually capable of devoting their lives to independent action are compelled by circumstances to renounce that course. As a rule they have to provide for one or more dependents, or they have to stay with their profession in order to earn a living. Only a person who, thanks to his own efforts or the devotion of friends, is free from material needs can nowadays take the risk of undertaking such a personal task.

This was not so much the case in earlier times because anyone who gave up remunerative work could still hope to get through life somehow or other, but anyone thinking of doing such a thing in the difficult economic conditions of today runs the risk of coming to grief both materially and spiritually.

I know not only by what I have observed but also by experience that there are worthy and capable people who have had to renounce a course of independent action that would have been of great value to the world because of circumstances that made it impossible.

Those who are given the chance to embark on a life of independent action must accept their good fortune in a spirit of humility. They must often think of those who, though equally willing and capable, were not in a position to do the same. And as a rule they must temper their own strong determination with humility. Almost always they must search and wait until they find a path that will permit the action they long to take. Fortunate are those who have received more years of creative work than years of searching and waiting. Fortunate those who succeed in giving themselves genuinely and completely.

These favored souls must also be humble so as not to get irritated by the resistance they encounter, but to accept it as inevitable. Anyone who proposes to do good must not expect people to roll any stones out of his way, and must calmly accept his lot even if they roll a few more into it. Only force that in the face of obstacles becomes stronger can win. Force that is used only to revolt wastes itself.

Of all the will toward the ideal in mankind only a small part can manifest itself in public action. All the rest of this force must be content with small and obscure deeds. The sum of these, however, is a thousand times stronger than the acts of those who receive wide public recognition. The latter, compared to the former, are like the foam on the waves of a deep ocean.

The hidden forces of goodness are alive in those who serve humanity as a secondary pursuit, those who cannot devote their full life to it. The lot of most people is to have a job, to earn their living, and to assume for themselves a place in society through some kind of nonfulfilling labor. They can give little or nothing of their human qualities. The problems arising from progressive specialization and mechanization of labor can only be partly resolved through the concessions society is willing to make in its economic planning. It is always essential that the individuals themselves not suffer their fate passively, but expend all their energies in affirming their own humanity through some spiritual engagement, even if the conditions are unfavorable.

One can save one's life as a human being, along with one's professional existence, if one seizes every oppor-

tunity, however unassuming, to act humanly toward those
who need another human being. In this way we serve both
the spiritual and the good. Nothing can keep us from this
second job of direct human service. So many opportunities
are missed because we let them pass by.

Everyone in his own environment must strive to practice
true humanity toward others. The future of the world depends on it.

Great values are lost at every moment because we miss
opportunities, but the values that are turned into will and
action constitute a richness that must not be undervalued.
Our humanity is by no means as materialistic as people
claim so complacently.

Judging by what I have learned about men and women,
I am convinced that far more idealistic aspiration exists than
is ever evident. Just as the rivers we see are much less
numerous than the underground streams, so the idealism
that is visible is minor compared to what men and women
carry in their hearts, unreleased or scarcely released. Mankind is waiting and longing for those who can accomplish
the task of untying what is knotted and bringing the underground waters to the surface.

What to my friends seemed most irrational in my plan
was that I wanted to go to Africa, not as a missionary, but
as a doctor. Already thirty years of age, I would burden
myself with long and laborious study. I never doubted for
an instant that these studies would require an immense
effort, and I anticipated the coming years with anxiety. But
the reasons that made me determined to enter into the
service I had chosen as a doctor weighed so heavily that
other considerations were as dust in the balance and
counted for nothing.

I wanted to be a doctor so that I might be able to work without having to talk. For years I had been giving of myself in words, and it was with joy that I had followed the calling of theological teacher and preacher. But this new form of activity would consist not in preaching the religion of love, but in practicing it. Medical knowledge would make it possible for me to carry out my intention in the best and most complete way, wherever the path of service might lead me.

Given my choice of equatorial Africa, acquiring this knowledge was especially appropriate because in the district to which I planned to go a doctor was, according to the missionaries' reports, the most urgent of all its needs. In their reports and magazines they always regretted that they could not provide help for the Africans who came in great physical pain. I was greatly motivated to study medicine and become, one day, the doctor whom these unhappy people needed. Whenever I was tempted to feel that the years I should have to sacrifice were too long, I reminded myself that Hamilcar and Hannibal had prepared for their march on Rome by their slow and tedious conquest of Spain.

There was still one more reason why it seemed to be my destiny to become a doctor. From what I knew of the Paris Missionary Society, I could not but feel very doubtful that they would accept me as a missionary.

It was in pietistic and orthodox circles that at the beginning of the nineteenth century societies were first formed for preaching the Gospel in the pagan world. About the same time, liberal Christendom also began to comprehend the need for carrying the teaching of Jesus to far-off lands. But when it came to action, orthodox Protestantism was first. It maintained lively and active organizations on the fringes of the main Church, and these were able to carry out their own independent activities. At that time the liberal Protestants were strong, but preoccupied with inner governmental problems in their Church. Moreover, the orthodox bodies with their pietistic ideas of "saving souls" had a stronger motive for mission work than did liberal Protestants. For them, the Gospel signified most of all a force for the regeneration of individual morality and for the human condition in general.

Once the missionary societies inspired by pietism and orthodoxy got to work they found support in liberal circles that were friendly to missions. These believed for a long time that they would not have to found their own missionary societies, but that by joining those in existence, all Protestants would eventually work together. They were mistaken, however. Indeed, the societies accepted all the material help offered them by liberal Protestantism—how hard my father and his liberal colleagues in Alsace had worked for missionary societies that had a quite different doctrinal outlook!—but they never sent out missionaries who would not accept their own doctrinal requirements.

Because liberal Protestantism did not organize missionary activities for a long time, it earned the reputation for neither realizing its importance nor doing anything about it. Finally it did found its own societies, but it was too late, and the hope that there could be one mission working in the name of the Protestant Church was lost.

I was always interested to discover that the missionaries themselves were more liberal in their thinking than the officials of their societies. Experience had, of course, taught them that in foreign lands, especially among the native people, the problem of dogmatic constraint versus liberalism that plagued European Christianity did not exist. The important thing out there is to preach the essentials of the Gospel as given in the Sermon on the Mount and to lead people to the spiritual realm of Jesus.

My father had a special sympathy for the Paris Missionary Society, because he thought he could detect in it a more liberal tendency than in the others. He particularly appreciated the fact that Casalis and others among its leading missionaries wrote their reports in straightforward language of a Christian character, rather than sugar-coated devotionals.

But I learned, and very definitely, that orthodoxy played the same role in the committee of the Paris Society that it did in others when I offered it my services. M. Boegner, the kindly director of the mission, was greatly moved upon finding that someone had offered to join the Congo mission in answer to his appeal, but at once confided to me that serious objections would be raised by members of the committee to my theological stance and that these would have to be removed first. My assurance that I wanted to come "merely as a doctor" lifted a heavy weight from his mind, but a little later he had to inform me that some members objected even to the acceptance of a mission doctor who subscribed only to proper Christian love, and did not, in their opinion, adhere to the correct Christian doctrine. However, we both resolved not to worry too much about the matter so far in advance, and thought the objectors still had some years during which they might arrive at a truly Christian understanding.

No doubt the more liberal Allgemeine Evangelische Missionsverein (General Union of Evangelical Missions) in Switzerland would have accepted me without hesitation either as missionary or doctor. But as I felt my call to equatorial Africa had come to me through the article in the Paris Missionary Society magazine, I felt I ought at least to try to join that mission's activities in that colony. Further,

I was curious to see whether a missionary society could justifiably arrogate the right to refuse the services of a doctor to the suffering people in their district because in their opinion he was not sufficiently orthodox.

But above and beyond all this, now that I was beginning my medical studies, my daily work and daily worries made such demands upon me that I had neither the time nor the strength to concern myself with what was to happen afterward.

My Medical Studies, 1905–1912

10

When I went to Professor Fehling, at that time dean of the department of medicine, to register as a student, he would have preferred to hand me over to his colleague in the psychiatric department.

On one of the closing days of October 1905, I set out in a thick fog to attend the first of a course of lectures on anatomy.

But there was still a legal question to resolve: I could not teach at the university and at the same time be enrolled as a student. Yet if I attended the medical courses only as an auditor,

I could not according to government rules be allowed to sit for examinations. The governing body met the difficulty in a friendly spirit, and permitted me to sit for the examinations on the strength of the affidavits the medical professors would give me certifying that I had attended their lectures. On their side, the professors resolved that, being a colleague, I might attend all the lectures without paying the fees.

My teachers in the five terms preceding the clinical were: Schwalbe, Weidenreich, and Fuchs in anatomy; Hofmeister, Ewald, and Spiro in physiology; Thiele in chemistry; Braun and Cohn in physics; Goette in zoology; Graf Solms and Jost in botany.

Now began years of continuous struggle with fatigue. I could not bring myself to give up either my teaching or my preaching. Thus, at the same time as I studied medicine, I was also delivering theological lectures and preaching almost every Sunday. My theology lectures were especially difficult at the beginning of my medical studies because I had begun to deal with the problems of the teaching of Paul.

The organ, too, began to absorb me now more than ever. For Gustave Bret (the conductor of the Paris Bach Society, which had been founded in 1905 by him, Dukas, Fauré, Widor, Guilmant, D'Indy, and myself) insisted on my undertaking the organ part in all the society's concerts. For some years, therefore, each winter I had to make several journeys to Paris. Although I had only to attend the final practice and could travel back to Strasbourg during the night following each performance, every concert took at least three days of my time. Many a sermon for St. Nicholai did I sketch out on the train between Paris and Strasbourg!

At Barcelona, too, I had to be at the organ for the Bach concerts at the Orfeó Catalá. And in general I now played more frequently in concerts, not only because I had become known as an organist in recent years but also because the loss of my stipend as principal of the theological college compelled me to find some other source of income.

The frequent journeys to Paris afforded me a welcome opportunity of meeting with friends whom I had made over the years in that city. Among those I knew best were the sensitive and musically gifted Frau Fanny Reinach, the wife of the well-known scholar Théodore Reinach, and Countess Mélanie de Pourtalès, the friend of the empress Eugénie, at whose side she figures in Winterhalter's famous picture. At the country house of the countess near Strasbourg, I frequently saw her friend Princess Metternich-Sandor, the wife of the Austrian ambassador to Paris in Napoleon III's days. It was she whom Wagner in his day had to thank for getting his *Tannhäuser* produced in the grand opera house at Paris. In the course of a conversation with Napoleon III during a ball, she procured the promise that he would give the order to include this opera in the list of works for performance. Under a somewhat pert exterior she concealed great intelligence and kindness of heart. I learned from her a good deal that was interesting about Wagner's stay in Paris and about the people who formed Napoleon's entourage. It was, however, not until I was in Africa and received her letters that the soul of this remarkable woman revealed itself to me.

While in Paris I also saw a good deal of Mlle Adèle Herrenschmidt, an Alsatian teacher.

I was attracted, at our first meeting, to Luis Millet, the conductor of the Orfeó Catalá, a first-rate artist and a man of thought. Through him I met the famous Catalonian architect Gaudí, who was at that time still fully occupied with his work on the peculiar Church of the Sagrada Familia (Holy Family), of which only a mighty portal, crowned with towers, had then been completed. Like architects of the Middle Ages, Gaudí began his work aware that it would take generations to finish. I shall never forget how in the builder's shed near the church, speaking as if he embodied the spirit of his countryman Ramón Lull, he introduced me to his mystical theory of proportions in architectural design that represent the Divine Trinity. "This cannot be expressed," he said, "in either French, German, or English, so I will explain it to you in Catalonian, and you will comprehend it, although you do not know the language."

As I was looking at *The Flight into Egypt*, carved in stone at the entrance of the big portal, and wondering at the donkey creeping along so wearily under its burden, he said to me: "You know something about art, and you feel that the donkey here is not an invention. Not one of the figures you see here in stone is imaginary; they all stand here just as I have seen them in reality: Joseph, Mary, the infant Jesus, the priests in the Temple; I chose them all from people I have met, and carved them from plaster casts that I took at the time. With the donkey it was a difficult job. When it became known that I was looking for an ass for *The Flight into Egypt*, they brought me all the finest donkeys in Barcelona. But I could not use them. Mary, with the child Jesus, was not to be mounted on a fine strong animal, but on a poor, old, and weary one, and surely one that had something kindly in its face and understood what it was all about. Such was the donkey I was looking for, and I found it at last hitched to the cart of a woman who was selling scouring sand. Its drooping head almost touched the ground. With much trouble I persuaded its owner to bring it to me. And then, as I copied it bit by bit in plaster of Paris, she kept crying because she thought it would not escape with its life. That is the donkey of *The Flight into Egypt*, and it has made an impression on you because it is not imagined, but from real life."

During the first months of my medical course I wrote the essay on organ building and the last chapters of *The Quest of the Historical Jesus*. I resigned my post as director of the theological seminary, where I had lived since my student years. Leaving the big trees in the walled-in garden, trees with which I had conversed for so many years while I was working, was very hard. But to my great joy I found that I should be able, after all, to stay on in the big house belonging to the Chapter of St. Thomas. Friedrich Curtius, first district superintendent of Colmar and then chosen, at the request of the whole body of Alsatian clergy, to be president of the Lutheran Church of Alsace, had taken possession of a large official residence in the chapter's big house. In it he offered me four small rooms in a top-floor apartment. Thus I was able to continue living under the shadow of St. Thomas. On the rainy Shrove Tuesday of 1906 the students carried my belongings out through one door of the house on the St. Thomas embankment and brought them back in through another.

With the Curtiuses I could come and go as if I were a member of the family, and that was most fortunate for me. Friedrich Curtius, who as we have said was a son of the well-known Greek scholar of Berlin, had married Countess

Louisa von Erlach, the daughter of the governess of the Grand Duchess Louisa von Baden, who was a sister of the emperor Frederick. In this family, traditions of the aristocracy of learning were united with those of the aristocracy of birth. The spiritual center of the household was the aged Countess von Erlach—born Countess de May from the area of Neuchâtel. Her health now prevented her from going out of doors, so in order to some extent to make up for her loss of concerts, which she felt very deeply for she was passionately fond of music, I used to play the piano to her for an hour every evening, and in that way I got to know her better; otherwise she scarcely saw anybody. This distinguished noblewoman gradually acquired a great influence over me, and I owe it to her that I have smoothed many rough edges off my personality.

On May 3, 1910, a pilot named Wincziers quite unexpectedly made the first flight over Strasbourg, from the parade grounds at Strasbourg-Neudorf. I happened to be in the countess's room at the time, and led her—for she could no longer move about alone—to the window. When the airplane, which had flown quite low past the house, had disappeared in the distance, she said to me in French, "Combien curieuse est ma vie! J'ai discuté les règles du participe passé avec Alexander von Humboldt, et voici que je suis témoin de la conquête de l'air par les hommes!" (How amazing is my life! I have discussed the rules of the past participle with Alexander von Humboldt, and here I am witnessing the conquest of the air by humans!")

Her two unmarried daughters, Ada and Greda von Erlach, who lived with her, had inherited from her a talent for painting, and while I was still director of the college I had given over to Ada, who was a pupil of Henner, a room with a northern exposure in my official residence to use as a studio. At her mother's request, I also sat for her as a model, since it was hoped that taking up painting again would help her recover from a severe operation, which had brought her temporary relief from an incurable and painful disease. She completed this picture of me on my thirtieth birthday, without any suspicion of anything that was stirring in my mind during that last sitting.

An uncle of the old Countess von Erlach had been for years an officer in the Dutch colonial service without suffering from fever, and he attributed this to his never having gone out of doors in the tropics bareheaded after sunset. I was made to promise that in her memory I would follow the same rule. So for her sake I now renounce the pleasure of letting the evening breeze play upon my head after a hot day on the Equator. Keeping my promise, however, has agreed with me. I have never had an attack of malaria, although of course the disease does not result from going out with an uncovered head in the tropics after sundown!

It was only from the spring of 1906 onward, when I had finished *The Quest of the Historical Jesus* and had given up the directorship of the seminary, that I could give to my new course of study the time it required. But then I worked with great zeal at the natural sciences. Now at last I was able to devote myself to what had attracted me most when I was at the Gymnasium: I was at last in a position to acquire the knowledge I needed in order to feel on firm ground in philosophy!

But the study of the natural sciences profited me even beyond the increase in knowledge I had longed for. It was an intellectual experience. All along I had felt it to be a danger that in the so-called humanities, with which I had hitherto been concerned, there is no truth that affirms itself as self-evident, but that a mere hypothesis can, by the way in which it is presented, be recognized as truth. The search for truth in the domain of the philosophy of history, for example, is an interminable sequence of duels between the sense of reality and creative power. Arguing from facts never wins a definitive victory against skillfully presented opinion. How often does what is perceived as progress consist in a skillfully formulated opinion that puts real insight out of action for a long time!

Having to watch this drama go on and on and having to deal in such different ways with men who had lost all feeling for reality had depressed me. Now I was suddenly in another land. I dealt with truths that embodied realities based on facts, and found myself among men who took it as a matter of course that they had to provide evidence before they made a statement. It was an experience I felt was needed for my own intellectual development.

Intoxicated as I was with the delight of dealing with realities that could be determined with exactitude, I was far from any inclination to undervalue the humanities, as others in a similar position often did. On the contrary. Through my study of chemistry, physics, zoology, botany, and physiology, I became aware more than ever of the extent to which truth in thought is justified and necessary, side by side with the truth that is established by facts. No doubt something subjective clings to the knowledge that results from the creative act of the mind. But at the same time such knowledge is on a higher plane than the knowledge based on facts alone.

The knowledge that results from the observation of diverse manifestations of being will always remain incomplete and unsatisfying because we cannot give a definite answer to the main question of what we are in the universe and to what purpose we exist in it. We can find our place in the existence that envelops us only if we experience in our individual lives the universal life that wills and rules within it. I can understand the nature of the living being outside of myself only through the living being within me. It is to this reflective knowledge of the universal being and of the relation to it of the individual human being that the humanities are devoted. The conclusions at which they arrive are determined by the sense of reality within the creative mind. Knowledge of reality must pass through a phase of thinking about the nature of being.

On May 13, 1908—the rainy day on which the famous Hohkönigsburg in Lower Alsace was ceremonially opened after its restoration—I took the examination in anatomy, physiology, and the natural sciences that has to be passed in order to begin medical and clinical courses. The acquisition of the necessary knowledge had cost me considerable effort. All my interest in the subject matter could not help me over the fact that the memory of a man over thirty no longer has the capacity of a twenty-year-old student's. Moreover, I had stupidly gotten into my head the idea of studying pure sciences exclusively, instead of preparing for the examination. It was only in the last few weeks that I followed the recommendations of my fellow students to become a member of a *Paukverband* (cramming club), so that I could get to know what sort of questions, according to the records kept by the students, the professors usually asked, together with the answers they preferred to hear.

The examination went better than I expected, even though during those days I was going through the worst crisis of exhaustion that I can recall during the whole of my life.

The terms of clinical study that followed proved far less of a strain than the earlier ones, because the various subjects were less diverse.

My principal teachers were: Moritz, Arnold Cahn, and Erich Meyer for medicine; Madelung and Ledderhose for surgery; Fehling and Freund for gynecology; Wollenberg, Rosenfeld, and Pfersdorff for psychiatry; Forster and Levy for bacteriology; Chiari for pathological anatomy; and Schmiedeberg for pharmacology.

I was especially interested in the lectures about drugs, where the practical instruction was given by Arnold Cahn, and the theoretical by Schmiedeberg, the well-known investigator into the derivatives of digitalis.

About Schmiedeberg and his friend Schwalbe, the anatomist, the following delightful story circulated at the university. Schwalbe was due to give a lecture on anthropology to the Adult Education Society of an Alsatian town and would of course have to mention the Darwinian theory. When he told Schmiedeberg of his fear that he might give offense, the latter replied: "Don't spare them! Tell them all about Darwinism, only take care not to use the word 'monkey,' and they'll be quite satisfied both with Darwin and with you." Schwalbe took the advice, and had the success that was promised.

At that time people in Alsace were beginning to demand

university extension courses to satisfy a population that was hungering for education, and one day Windelband, the professor of philosophy, announced to us in the common room with joyful astonishment that a deputation of workingmen had requested that he give some lectures on Hegel. He could hardly speak warmly enough of the way people without higher education, with their healthy feeling for what is really valuable, had awakened to the importance of Hegel. Later on, however, it came out that what they wanted to hear was something about Ernst Haeckel and the materialistic popular philosophy akin to socialism that was expounded in his book *The Riddle of the Universe*, which appeared in 1899. In their Alsatian pronunciation the *ae* had sounded like *e*, and the *k* like *g*!

Years later I was able to render a service to Schmiedeberg, whom I greatly admired. In the spring of 1919 I happened to be passing the Strasbourg-Neudorf station, from which some Germans whom the French authorities had decided to expel were about to be transported, when I saw the dear old man standing among them. To my question as to whether I could help him to save his furniture, which like the rest he had been obliged to leave behind, he replied by showing me a parcel wrapped in newspaper, which he had under his arm. It was his last work on digitalin. Since everything that these expelled people had on them or with them was strictly examined by French officials at the railway station, he was afraid that he might not be allowed to take with him the bulky parcel with his manuscript. I therefore took it from him and sent it later on, when a safe opportunity arose, to Baden-Baden, where he had found a refuge with friends. He died not long after his book appeared in print.

At the beginning of my medical course I had to struggle

with lack of money, but my position improved later on owing to the success of the German edition of my book on Bach and the concert fees I earned.

In October 1910, I took the state medical examination. I had earned the fee for it the previous month at the French Music Festival at Munich by playing the organ part of Widor's recently completed *Sinfonia Sacra*, with him conducting the orchestra. On December 2, after my last examination, with Madelung, the surgeon, I strode out of the hospital into the darkness of the winter evening, unable to grasp the fact that the terrible strain of my medical studies was now behind me. Again and again I had to assure myself that I was really awake and not dreaming. Madelung's voice seemed to come from some distant sphere when he said more than once as we walked along together, "It is only because you have such excellent health that you have got through a job like that."

Now I had to complete a year of practical work as an intern in the hospitals and to write my thesis for the doctorate. As my subject I chose a critical review of all that had been published about the mental illness from which Jesus was supposed to have suffered.

In the main I was concerned with the works of De Loosten, William Hirsch, and Binet-Sanglé. In my studies on the life of Jesus I had documented that he lived in the world of contemporary Judaic thought, which seems fantastic to us now, with the expectation of the end of the world and the appearance of a supernatural Messianic Kingdom. I was immediately reproached for making Him a visionary, or even a person under the sway of delusions. Now my task was to decide whether, from a medical standpoint, this peculiar Messianic consciousness of His was in any way bound up with some psychic disturbance.

De Loosten, William Hirsch, and Binet-Sanglé had assumed some paranoiac mental disturbance in Jesus and had
discovered in Him morbid ideas about His own greatness
and His persecution. In order to deal with their really quite
insignificant works, it was necessary to immerse myself in
the boundless problem of paranoia. As a result a treatise
of forty-six pages took over a year to write. More than once
I was on the point of throwing it aside and choosing another
subject for my dissertation.

The result I had in mind was to demonstrate that the
only psychiatric characteristics that could be considered
historical, and about which there could be any serious dispute—Jesus' high estimation of Himself and possible hal-
lucinations at the time of His baptism—were far from
sufficient to prove the presence of any mental disease.

The expectation of the end of the world and the coming
of the Messianic Kingdom has nothing in it in the nature
of a delusion, for it belonged to a view of the world that
was widely accepted by the Jews of that time and was
contained in their religious literature. Even the idea held
by Jesus that He was the One who would be manifested as
the Messiah upon the appearance of the Messianic Kingdom contains no trace of a morbid delusion of grandeur. If
family tradition convinced Him that He was of the House
of David, He may well have thought Himself justified in
claiming for Himself one day the Messianic dignity promised to a descendant of David in the writings of the prophets. If He chose to keep secret His certainty that He was
the coming Messiah and nevertheless let a glimmer of the
truth break through in His discourses, His action, viewed
solely from the outside, is not unlike that of persons with
a morbid delusion of grandeur. But in reality it is something
quite different. Concealing His claim had in His case a
natural and logical foundation. According to Jewish doctrine
the Messiah would not step forth out of His concealment

until the Messianic Kingdom had been revealed. Jesus therefore could not make Himself known to men as the coming Messiah. And if, on the other hand, an announcement of the coming of the Kingdom of God turns up in a number of His sayings, made with all the authority of Him who is to be its King, that, too, is thoroughly intelligible from a logical point of view. Jesus never behaved like a man lost in a world of illusions. He reacted in an absolutely normal fashion to what was said to Him, and to the events that concerned Him. He was never out of touch with reality.

That these medical experts succeed in casting doubt on the medical soundness of Jesus, in the face of the simplest psychiatric considerations, is explicable only by their not being sufficiently familiar with the historical side of the question. Not only do they fail to use the late Jewish view of the world in explaining the world of ideas in which Jesus lived, but they also fail to distinguish the historical from the unhistorical statements that we have about Him. Instead of keeping to what is recorded in the two oldest sources, Mark and Matthew, they bring together everything that is said in the four Gospels collectively, and then sit in judgment on a personality that is in reality fictitious and consequently can be viewed as abnormal. It is significant that the chief arguments for the mental unsoundness of Jesus are drawn from the Gospel of John.

In reality Jesus was convinced of His being the coming Messiah because, amid the religious ideas then prevalent, His powerful ethical personality could not have done otherwise than to arrive at an awareness of itself within the frame of this idea. By his spiritual nature He was in fact the ethical master promised by the prophets.

Preparing for Africa

11

While I was still working on the dissertation for my medical degree, I had already begun making preparations for my journey to Africa. In the spring of 1912 I gave up teaching at the university and my post at St. Nicholai. The lecture courses I gave in the winter of 1911–1912 dealt with attempts to reconcile a religious view of the world with the results of historical research on world religions and with the facts of natural science.

My last sermon to the congregation of St. Nicholai used as its text Paul's blessing in his Epistle to the Philippians: "The peace of God which passeth all understanding, shall keep your hearts and minds in Christ Jesus," a text I used to close every service I had held all through the years.

Not to preach anymore, not to lecture anymore, was a great sacrifice. Until I left for Africa I avoided going past either St. Nicholai or the university as much as I could, because I found too painful the very sight of the places where I had carried on work I could never resume. To this day I cannot bear to look at the windows that belong to the second classroom to the east of the entrance to the great university building, because it was there that I most often lectured.

Finally, with my wife—Helene Bresslau, the daughter of the Strasbourg historian, whom I had married on June 18, 1912—I left my home on the St. Thomas embankment so that I might spend in my father's parsonage at Günsbach as much time in the last months as my travels allowed. My wife had already been a valuable collaborator in completing manuscripts and correcting proofs before our marriage, and she was again a great help with all the work dealing with my publications that had to be completed before we started for Africa.

I had spent the spring of 1912 in Paris studying tropical medicine and making a start at purchasing the supplies that would be needed for Africa. Although I acquired a theoretical knowledge of my subject at the beginning of my medical studies, it was now time to work at it from a practical point of view. This, too, was a new experience. Until then I had engaged only in intellectual labor. Now I had to make lists of things to be ordered from catalogues, go shopping for days on end, stand about in the shops looking for what I wanted, check accounts and delivery notes, fill packing cases, prepare accurate lists for customs inspections, and busy myself with other such tasks.

How much time and trouble it cost me to get together the instruments, the drugs, the bandages, and all the other articles needed to equip a hospital, not to mention all the work we did together to prepare for housekeeping in the primeval forest!

At first I regarded dealing with these things to be something of a burden. By now, however, I have reached the point where I derive aesthetic pleasure from the careful preparation of a list of things to be ordered. The irritation I do feel again and again comes from the fact that so many catalogues, including those of pharmaceutical products, are arranged as inconsistently and inconveniently as if the firm in question had entrusted their compilation to its doorman's wife.

To finance my undertaking, I began a round of soliciting visits among my acquaintances and experienced in full measure the difficulty of winning support for work that had not yet justified its existence with results. Most of my friends and acquaintances helped me over this embarrassment by offering help for my adventurous plan on the grounds that I was its author. But I must confess to having also had the experience of sensing the tone of my reception change markedly when it became apparent that I was there, not on a social call, but to raise money. Still, the kindness I encountered on these rounds outweighed a hundredfold the humiliations I had to accept.

That the German professors at the University of Strasbourg gave so liberally to an enterprise destined for a

French colony moved me deeply. A considerable portion of the total I received came from members of my congregation at St. Nicholai. I was also supported by the Alsatian parishes, especially those whose pastors had been my fellow students or pupils. Money for the project to be established also flowed in from a benefit concert the Paris Bach Society gave in its behalf with its choir, supported by Maria Philippi and myself. A concert and a lecture in Le Havre—where I was known through my participation in a Bach concert— were also a great financial success.

Thus the financial problem was solved for the present. I had money enough for all the purchases needed for the voyage and for running the hospital for about a year. Well-to-do friends had indicated, moreover, that they would help me again when I had exhausted my present resources.

I was given valuable help in the management of financial and business matters by Mrs. Annie Fischer, the widow of a professor of surgery at the University of Strasbourg who had died young. Subsequently she took upon herself all the work that had to be done in Europe while I was in Africa. Later on, her son also became a doctor in the tropics.

When I was certain I could collect sufficient funds to establish a small hospital, I made a definite offer to the Paris Missionary Society to come at my own expense to serve its mission field on the river Ogowé from the centrally located station at Lambaréné.

The mission station at Lambaréné was established in 1876 by Dr. Nassau, an American missionary and medical man. The missionary work in the Ogowé district had been started by American missionaries who had come to the country in

1874. Somewhat later the Gaboon became a French possession, and from 1892 onward the Paris Missionary Society replaced the American, since the Americans were not able to comply with the requirement of the French government that all instruction in schools be given in French.

M. Boegner's successor as superintendent of missions, M. Jean Bianquis, whose piety of deeds, rather than words, and able management of the society's affairs won him many friends, maintained with all the weight of his authority that they must not lose this opportunity of obtaining, free of cost, the mission doctor for whom they had so ardently longed. But the strictly orthodox objected. It was resolved to invite me to appear before the committee so they could examine my beliefs. I could not agree to this, basing my refusal on the fact that Jesus, when He called His disciples, required from them nothing more than the will to follow Him. I also sent a message to the committee that, if the saying of Jesus, "He who is not against us is for us," is a command to be followed, then a missionary society errs if it rejects even a Muslim who offers his services for the treatment of the suffering native people. Not long before this the society rejected a minister who wanted to come work for them, because his theological convictions did not allow him to answer the question, Did he regard the fourth Gospel as the work of the Apostle John? with an unqualified yes.

To avoid a similar fate I declined to appear before the assembled committee and allow them to put theological questions to me. As an alternative, I offered to visit each member of the committee personally, so that conversation might allow each to judge clearly whether accepting me would really pose such a terrible threat to the souls of the

Africans and to the society's reputation. My proposal was accepted, and it cost me several afternoons. A few of the members gave me a chilly reception. The majority assured me that my theological point of view made them hesitate chiefly for two reasons: I might be tempted to confuse the missionaries out there with my learning, and I might wish to be active again as a preacher. My assurances that I only wanted to be a doctor, and that on every other topic I would be *muet comme une carpe* (dumb as a carp), allayed their fears, and these visits actually helped establish quite cordial relations with a number of the committee members.

In the end my offer was accepted on the understanding that I would avoid everything that could cause offense to the missionaries and to the faith of their converts. One member of the committee did, however, send in his resignation.

One more thing now remained to be done, namely, I still had to secure permission to practice as a doctor in the Gaboon from the Colonial Department, because I only had a German diploma. With the help of influential acquaintances this last obstacle was removed. Finally the road was clear!

In February 1913, the seventy packing cases were closed and sent in advance to Bordeaux by freight train. While we were packing our hand luggage, my wife began to object to my insistence that we take with us two thousand marks in gold instead of in notes. I replied that we must reckon on the possibility of war, and that if war broke out gold would retain its value in every country in the world, whereas the fate of paper money was uncertain and bank credits might be frozen.

I took into consideration the danger of war because I had

learned from acquaintances in Paris who had friends at the Russian embassy that war might break out as soon as Russia had completed the strategic railways she was building in Poland.

I was quite convinced, indeed, that neither the French people nor the Germans wanted war and that the parliamentary leaders of both nations were eager for opportunities to get together and give expression to their ideas. As someone who had been working for years to bring about an understanding between Germany and France, I knew how much was being done at that very time to preserve the peace, and I had some hope of success. On the other hand, I never shut my eyes to the fact that the fate of Europe did not depend upon Franco-German relations alone.

It seemed to me an ominous sign that in Germany, as in France, gold was being withdrawn from circulation whenever possible and replaced by paper money. Beginning in 1911 civil servants in both countries scarcely ever received gold when they were paid their salaries. Until that time German officials had been allowed to choose whether their salary would be paid in gold or in paper.

Literary Studies During My Medical Course

12   In the last two years of my medical studies and during the time I spent as a hospital intern, by severely limiting my night's rest I managed to complete a work on the history of research on the Apostle Paul and to revise and enlarge *The Quest of the Historical Jesus* for a second edition. In addition Widor and I worked on an edition of Bach's preludes and fugues for the organ, with directions for the interpretation of each piece.

Immediately after completing *The Quest of the Historical Jesus* I began to study the teachings of Paul. From the very beginning I had been dissatisfied with explanations in scholarly theology because they represented Paul's thought as complicated, contradictory, and incompatible with his originality and greatness. From the time I realized that the preaching of Jesus had been entirely determined by the expectation of the imminent end of the world and of the advent of the supernatural Kingdom of God, I began to question this view.

Now I had to ask myself the question that previous research had not: Was Paul's thought also rooted in eschatology? I quickly came to the conclusion that it was. In 1906 I had already lectured on the eschatological concepts that serve as a basis for the strange Pauline doctrine of our being united with Christ and of death and resurrection with Him.

In this inquiry I wanted to familiarize myself with all the attempts that had thus far been made to find a historical explanation for the Pauline doctrine. I hoped to show clearly how the whole complex of questions had gradually evolved. I proceeded in the same way with my investigation into Paul's teachings as I had with my studies of the Last Supper and for *The Quest of the Historical Jesus*. Instead of contenting myself with simply providing a solution, I took it upon myself to investigate and write the history of the problem. That I thrice attempted to pursue this laborious detour is the fault of Aristotle. How often have I cursed the hour when I first read the section of his *Metaphysics* where he explores the problem of philosophy through a criticism of earlier philosophizing! These pages awakened in me something that had been long dormant. Since then I have experienced over and over again that compulsion to grasp the nature of a problem not only as it now stands but by tracing its evolution through history.

Whether the amount of labor justifies the effort I have put into it, I do not know. I am certain only of one thing: I had no choice but to proceed in this Aristotelian fashion, and it brought me intellectual satisfaction and aesthetic pleasure.

I was particularly attracted to the history of critical studies of Pauline teaching because investigation of it was a task no one had yet undertaken, and the University of Strasbourg had special resources available, for it contained almost as many books on Paul as on the life of Jesus. In addition, the head librarian, Dr. Schorbach, helped me find all the books as well as journal articles on the subject.

Originally I believed that this literary-historical study could briefly be treated as a chapter introducing an exposition of the eschatological significance of Paul's thought, but as I worked along, it became clear that it would develop into an entire book.

Scholarly investigation of Paul's thought begins with Hugo Grotius. In his *Annotationes in Novum Testamentum*, which appeared around the middle of the seventeenth century, he states the self-evident principle that in order to understand the Epistles of Paul, we must know the proper meaning of their words. In the past, both Catholic and Protestant theologians interpreted Paul in accordance with the doctrine of justification by faith.

The idea that the passages about his being in Christ and having died and risen with Him pose important problems had never entered the minds of the representatives of the new historical criticism. For them it was most important to show that Paul's teaching was not dogmatic, but "conforms to reason."

The first achievement of Pauline research was to establish the differences in thought that distinguish individual Epistles from each other. This led to the conclusion that some of the Epistles could not be accepted as authentic.

In 1807 Schleiermacher expressed his doubts about the genuineness of the First Epistle to Timothy. Seven years later Johann Gottfried Eichorn proved with convincing arguments that neither the Epistles to Timothy nor that to Titus could have come from Paul's own hand. Then Ferdinand Christian Baur of Tübingen University went further still in his *Paulus der Apostel Jesu Christi (Paul the Apostle of Jesus Christ)*, which appeared in 1845. He recognized only the two Epistles to the Corinthians and those to the Romans and the Galatians as indisputably genuine. Except for these, all the others appeared to him to be more or less questionable.

Later research has modified the severity of this judgment, though it is in principle correct. It has revealed that the Epistles to the Philippians, to Philemon, and the First Epistle to the Thessalonians are also authentic. Thus the majority of the Epistles bearing Paul's name can be attributed to him. Contemporary historical criticism considers the Second Epistle to the Thessalonians, that to Titus, and the two to Timothy as definitely apocryphal. About the Epistles to the Ephesians and the Colossians a definitive judgment is not yet possible. They contain thoughts that are closely allied with those of the genuine Epistles but differ markedly from them in detail.

Baur found a criterion for distinguishing the genuine from the nongenuine in the contrast he discovered between the belief Paul held about Christ and that held by the Apostles at Jerusalem. He was the first bold enough to state that the Epistle to the Galatians is a polemical treatise directed against the Apostles at Jerusalem. He was also the first to recognize that the difference of opinion concerning the authority of the Law in Christianity arises from the varying significance given to the death of Jesus. When this contrast became clear, Baur could conclude that the Epistles in which the death of Jesus brings about a change in this world came from Paul himself. The others were written by disciples who wanted to attribute the later reconciliation between the two parties to Paul's own time.

By distinguishing between the Pauline Epistles, Baur was the first to pose the question concerning the formation of Christian dogma. He correctly saw that the rapid diffusion of Paul's ideas can be attributed to his belief that the death of Christ signified the end of the Law. In the course of one or two generations this concept became the common property of the Christian faith, although it stood in contradiction to the traditional teaching represented by the Apostles at Jerusalem.

By recognizing that the problem of Pauline teaching forms the core of the problem of the origins of Christian dogma, Baur initiated a flood of historical research into the beginnings of Christianity. Before his time it had made no progress because its task had not been properly formulated.

Edouard Reuss, Otto Pfleiderer, Karl Holsten, Ernest Renan, H. J. Holtzmann, Karl von Weizsäcker, Adolf von Harnack, and others who continued the work of Baur in the second half of the nineteenth century studied the various elements of Pauline teaching with great care. They all agree that, in addition to the doctrine of redemption through sacrifice, there is in Paul's thought another doctrine of an entirely different character. According to this doctrine, believers themselves experience in a mysterious way the death and resurrection of Jesus and thereby become new beings, ruled by the power of the spirit of Jesus. The fundamental thoughts of this mystical-ethical doctrine are expressed for the first time in Herrmann Lüdemann's *Anthropology of St. Paul*, published in 1872.

To resolve the Pauline problem one must explain why Paul claims that the Law is no longer valid for Christians, and why along with the doctrine of redemption by faith in the atoning death of Jesus, which he holds in common with the Apostles in Jerusalem, Paul professes belief in a mystical union with Christ, through whom we die and rise again.

Historical criticism at the end of the nineteenth and the beginning of the twentieth century thought that it could explain Paul's views as having advanced beyond those of primitive Christianity because of his background. Born and educated in Tarsus in Asia Minor, where society was entirely under the influence of Greek language and civilization, he combined Hellenistic and Jewish thought. As a result of this combination, he became an opponent of the Law. He also tried to prove that redemption through the death of Jesus is not only based on the Jewish concept of sacrifice but can be understood as a mystical participation in this death.

This solution to the problem seems the most obvious and natural in view of the fact that mystical thought is unknown to Judaism, but quite common in the Greek world. The hypothesis that the Pauline doctrine of redemption is essentially Greek has been reinforced by abundant documentation since the beginning of the twentieth century. Hermann Usener, E. Rhode, François Cumont, Hugo Hepding, Richard Reitzenstein, and others examined Greek literature and newly discovered inscriptions from the first centuries A.D. that until then had been only superficially examined. These new sources revealed the role sacramental rites played in religious life at the beginning of Greco-Oriental decadence. The hypothesis that the mysticism of Paul is somehow determined by Greek religiosity seems best explained by the fact that in Paul's view the believer actually participates in the death and resurrection of Jesus through baptism and the Lord's Supper. They were not merely symbols as people at the end of the nineteenth century had thought before it was realized that Paul really thought along sacramental lines.

Since Judaism was as little familiar with sacraments as it was with mysticism, it was thought necessary to establish a link between Paul and Greek religiosity to account for his view of baptism and the Last Supper. Much as this hypothesis has in its favor at first glance, it is insufficient as an explanation for the mysticism of Paul concerning our union with Christ. As soon as the assumption is examined in detail it becomes evident that the ideas of Paul are quite different in character from those of the Greco-Oriental mystery religions. Essentially they are not even related, though there is a remarkable resemblance between them.

If Paul's doctrine of mystical redemption and his sacramental views cannot be explained as stemming from Hellenistic ideas, the only other possible course is to view them in the context of the late Jewish view of the end of the world, i.e., of eschatology. This course is followed by Richard Kabisch, in *The Eschatology of St. Paul in Its Connection with the Whole Idea of Paulinism* (1893), and by William Wrede, in his *St. Paul* (1904), which unfortunately remained a preliminary sketch. Neither of them was able to give a complete explication of Paul's system of thought, but they did provide the most convincing evidence that within the framework of eschatology many Pauline concepts that seemed disjointed not only were in fact simple and viable but constituted an entirely coherent system in their relation to one another.

These investigations, conducted outside of contemporary criticism, did not attract attention because the theory that Paul combined Greek and Jewish thought seemed evident to theologians and other scholars of Hellenism in the first centuries A.D. They failed to see the danger to which they exposed the unfortunate Apostle by their assertion that the essential ideas of the Epistles that bear his name appear to be like those of the Greco-Oriental religions of the second and third centuries A.D.! The inevitable question also arises as to whether these letters really belong to the fifties and sixties of the first Christian century, or whether they originated in a later period and were only attributed to the rabbi Paul of primitive Christianity through a literary fiction.

In the second half of the nineteenth century Bruno Bauer and certain adherents of the so-called radical Dutch school—A. D. Loman, Rudolph Steck, W. C. van Manen, and others—proclaimed that the Greek ideas in the letters bearing Paul's name are much easier to explain if it is recognized that the writings are actually of Greek origin, rather than assuming that a rabbi gave a new Greek character to primitive Christian beliefs immediately after the death of Jesus. They assert that the struggle against the Law cannot have been undertaken by the rabbi Paul.

The demand for freedom from the Law must first have been expressed when the Greeks became the dominant influence in the Christian communities and rebelled against a Christianity that had been shaped by Judaism. The struggle over the Law, therefore, must have been fought, not in the middle of the first century between Paul and the Apostles in Jerusalem, but two or three generations later between the two parties that had come into existence in the intervening period. To legitimize their victory the independents supposedly attributed the Epistles to Paul and published them under his name. This paradoxical theory of the origin of the Pauline letters cannot, of course, be historically proved. It does, however, reveal quite strikingly the difficulties in which research finds itself when it assumes the existence of Greek thought in Paul's work.

To conclude the history of critical research into Paul's thought, I felt obliged, in 1911, to explain that the idea that the Apostle's mystical redemption was not Jewish but

Hellenistic could not be sustained. The only plausible explanation could be found in eschatology.

When these introductory investigations appeared in print my full exposition of the eschatological origin of Paul's thought was so near completion that I could have given it to the publisher within a few weeks. But these weeks were not at my disposal, since I had to begin to study for the state medical examination. Later on, so much of my time was taken up by my doctoral dissertation and the revision of *The Quest of the Historical Jesus* that I had to give up all hope of publishing the second part of my work on Paul before my departure for Africa.

In the autumn of 1912, when I was already busy shopping and packing for Lambaréné, I undertook to integrate into *The Quest of the Historical Jesus* material from the new books that had in the meantime appeared on the subject and to rewrite sections that no longer satisfied me. I especially wanted to explain late Jewish eschatology more thoroughly and to discuss the works of John M. Robertson, William Benjamin Smith, James George Frazer, Arthur Drews, and others, who contested the historical existence of Jesus.

It is not difficult to pretend that Jesus never lived. The attempt to prove it, however, invariably produces the opposite conclusion. In the Jewish literature of the first century the existence of Jesus is not attested to with any certainty, and in the Greek and Latin literature of the same period there is no evidence for it at all. Of the two passages in his *Antiquities* in which the Jewish writer Josephus makes incidental mention of Jesus, one was undoubtedly interpolated by Christian copyists. The first pagan witness to His existence is Tacitus, who, during the reign of Trajan in the second decade of the second century A.D., reports in his *Annals* (XV.44) that the founder of the "Christian" sect (which Nero accused of causing the great fire at Rome) was executed under the government of Tiberius by the procurator of Judea, Pontius Pilate.

Since Roman history mentions the existence of Jesus only as the reason for the persistence of the Christian movement, and this for the first time about eighty years after the death of Jesus, and since some critics accept the thesis that neither the Gospels nor the Epistles are authentic, anyone can consider himself justified in refusing to recognize the historical existence of Jesus.

But that does not settle the matter. It still has to be explained when, where, and how Christianity originated without either Jesus or Paul; how it later on came to trace its origins back to these mythical personalities; and finally for what curious reasons they, both Jewish, were designated as the founders of Christianity.

To prove that the Gospels and Epistles are not genuine one has to explain how they were written without being authentic. The champions of the thesis that Jesus is not a historical person give no account of the difficulty their view presents; they treat the matter too casually. Though they differ considerably from each other in details, the method they all apply involves attempts to prove that in pre-Christian times, in Palestine or elsewhere in the East, a Christ cult or Jesus cult of a Gnostic character already existed, which, as in the cults of Adonis, Osiris, and Tammuz, centered on a god or demigod who dies and rises again.

Since any proof of such a pre-Christian Christ cult is

lacking, its existence must be made to appear probable by a combination of inventions. Through further acts of invention and imagination it is then shown that the adherents of this assumed pre-Christian Christ cult at some point had reason to change the god who dies and rises again into a historical human personality.

As if this were not difficult enough, the Gospels and the Pauline Epistles require an explanation as to why their Christ cult, instead of having originated in a past age of unverifiable events, happened to date its imaginary Jesus scarcely two or three generations back and had him enter history as a Jew among Jews.

Finally, their most arduous task consists in explaining how the content of the Gospels turned from myth into history. If they keep to their theory, Drews, Smith, and Robertson must maintain that the events and the words reported by Matthew and Mark are only the ideas professed by earlier mystery religions. The fact that Arthur Drews and others refer not only to every myth they can find but also to astronomy and astrology in order to justify this explanation shows the strain they put on our imagination.

It is clear, then, from the writings of those who dispute the historicity of Jesus, that the hypothesis of His existence is a thousand times easier to prove than that of His nonexistence. But that does not mean that this hopeless undertaking has been abandoned. Again and again books about the nonexistence of Jesus appear and find credulous readers, although they contain nothing new beyond what Robertson, Smith, Drews, and the other supporters of this thesis have said. The supporters of this thesis have to be satisfied with passing off old arguments as new.

As far as these attempts aspire to serve the cause of

historical truth, they can claim that the rapid acceptance throughout the Greek world of a doctrine that had its roots in Judaism (as recorded in the traditional history of the beginnings of Christianity) is difficult to explain and that therefore the hypothesis of the derivation of Christianity from Greek thought merits further attention.

But this hypothesis cannot be sustained. It breaks down because nothing about the person of Jesus in the first two Gospels could possibly be explained as originating in myth. In addition, the eschatology of Jesus has a peculiar character that a later period could not have attributed to a person of its own invention; the good reason is that the generation that preceded the destruction of the Temple by Titus did not know enough about Jewish eschatology, and the contemporaries of Jesus did. What interest could this so-called mystery cult of Christ have in attributing to this pseudo-historical Jesus whom it invented the belief—not confirmed by fact—in the imminent end of the world and the coming of the Messiah, the Son of Man?

By his eschatology Jesus is so completely and firmly rooted in the period in which the two oldest Gospels place Him that He can only be represented as a personality that really appeared in that period. It is significant that those who dispute the historical existence of Jesus prudently avoid examining his thought and action as determined by eschatology.

A request from Widor had me occupied again with Bach before I left for Africa. The New York publisher Mr. G. Schirmer had asked him to prepare an edition of Bach's organ works with some notes on their interpretation. Widor agreed on the condition that I would collaborate. So we divided the task: I was to prepare the rough drafts on which we would then work together. How many times in 1911 and 1912 did I travel to Paris to devote myself to our work! Widor twice spent several days with me in Günsbach that we might concentrate on this task in undisturbed quiet.

Although as a matter of principle we both disapproved of so-called practical editions, which prescribe rules to the player, we nevertheless believed that for Bach's organ music some advice was justifiable. With few exceptions, Bach gave no directions in his organ compositions for registration or change of manuals. It was unnecessary for the organists of his day. The pieces were rendered as Bach had intended as a result of the way the organs were constructed and customarily played.

Soon after Bach's death his organ compositions, which he had never published, were practically forgotten for a long time. When, thanks to the Peters edition, they were rediscovered in the middle of the nineteenth century, musical taste and organs had both changed. The eighteenth-century tradition was known, but its style of rendering Bach's organ works in that way was rejected as too simple and too plain. It was believed that one was acting in his spirit if one used the constant changes in volume and character of sound made possible by the contemporary organ. As a result, toward the end of the nineteenth century modern organ playing had so completely supplanted the earlier method that it never received any attention, if indeed anyone still knew what it had been.

France was an exception. Widor, Guilmant, and the rest held firmly to the old German tradition, which had been transmitted to them by the well-known organist Adolph

Friedrich Hesse (1802–1863) of Breslau. The reason was that until about the middle of the nineteenth century, there was in fact no art of organ playing in France, because the organs that had been destroyed during the Revolution had for the most part been only poorly restored. Until Cavaillé-Col and others began to build their fine instruments and the German Peters edition enabled organists to acquire Bach's organ compositions, they did not know—so Widor often told me—how to play something so completely unknown in France. They were unfamiliar with the music and had to learn an entirely new pedal technique. It was Lemmens, the well-known organist in Brussels, to whom they went, and Cavaillé-Col paid the expenses for those who could not have afforded to go on their own. Lemmens had been a pupil of Adolph Friedrich Hesse, the organist in Breslau, Germany, who had studied in the tradition of Bach with his teacher, Kittel.

At the inauguration of the newly built organ at St. Eustache's in 1844, thanks to Hesse the Parisians heard Bach's organ music for the first time. In the years that followed, Hesse was often invited to France that he might be heard at the inauguration of other organs. His playing at the Universal Exposition in London in 1854 did much to make Bach's music known in England.

If the French organists clung to the German tradition transmitted by Hesse and Lemmens, it was a matter not only of taste but of technical exigency. The organs built by Cavaillé-Col were not modern organs. They did not have the mechanical means that made possible the variety in registration of the German nineteenth-century organs. The French organists were forced to play in the classical tradition. This, however, was no drawback, because the wonderful sonority of their organs allowed the Bach fugues to achieve the full effect of the organs of Bach's own day, without resorting to special changes in registration.

Thus by a historical paradox the principles of the old German tradition were preserved for the present age by Parisian organists. This tradition also became known in detail when by degrees musicians again began to consult the theoretical works of the eighteenth century.

For anyone who looked, as I did, for every possible opportunity to play Bach on instruments of his own time, these organs were the true masters of the faithful interpretation of Bach's music. They demonstrated what was technically possible, as well as the musical effects that could be achieved.

For the new edition we were preparing, Widor and I thought that our task consisted in explaining to organists who only knew modern organs and were ignorant of Bach's style what registration and what changes of keyboard Bach had to use. In addition, we wanted to consider to what extent the original style could be retained by using the sound and the tone colors of the modern organ.

We thought tact demanded that we not insert our own directions or suggestions in the musical score itself. We decided instead to include our comments in short articles as introductions to the individual pieces. The organist may then read our suggestions but play Bach without any cicerone. We did not even include fingering or phrasing.

Bach's fingering differs from ours in that he crosses any finger over another, following an older fashion, and therefore uses the thumb less frequently. In pedaling Bach could not use the heel because the pedals of his day were short and he had to use the toe of the foot. The shortness of the pedals also made it difficult to pass one foot over the other. He was therefore often obliged to let his foot glide from one pedal to the next, whereas we can manage a better legato than was possible for him by moving one foot over the other, or by using toe and heel alternately.

When I was young I still found the short pedal of the Bach period on many old village organs. Even today in Holland many pedals are so short that it is impossible to use the heel.

Widor and I put our remarks concerning matters of phrasing into the introduction because I am always irritated when I encounter the fingering and the phrasing of some editor or other. I insisted on the principle, which, it is to be hoped, will someday be universally accepted, that the player must have before his eyes the music of Bach or Mozart or Beethoven as it was written by the composer himself.

A few concessions to modern taste and to modern organs had to be made because Bach's music, as he had conceived it, cannot be played on our modern instruments. On the instruments of his day the forte and the fortissimo were relatively soft, so a piece could be played entirely in fortissimo, and the listener still did not tire or feel any need of change. Similarly, Bach could impose on his hearers a continual forte with his orchestra. On modern organs, the fortissimo is usually so loud and so harsh that the listener cannot endure it for more than a few moments. Furthermore, he is not able to follow the individual lines of melody, amid all the roar, and this is essential for understanding a Bach composition. We are therefore obliged to play some passages with varying color and intensity that Bach would have played entirely in forte or fortissimo if the listener is to enjoy the music.

Nothing can be said against variations in intensity that Bach could not achieve on the organs of his time as long as the architecture of the piece remains clearly perceptible and if it does not seem restless. Where Bach was satisfied to carry a fugue through with three or four degrees of tonality, we can allow ourselves six or eight. The supreme rule for the execution of Bach's organ works is that the design must be clear; the tone color is less important.

The organist must always remind himself that the listener can only perceive the design of the composition when the lines of melody are perfectly distinct. That is why Widor and I emphasize again and again that the performer must be clear about the phrasing of the various themes and motifs of the pieces and bring out all details with the same clarity.

One cannot be reminded too often that on the organs of the eighteenth century it was not possible to play as rapidly as one might have wished. The keys were so stiff and had to be depressed so hard that a good moderato was in itself something of an achievement. Because Bach must have conceived his preludes and fugues in the moderate tempo in which they could be played on his own organs, we too must hold fast to this fact and perform them in an authentic and appropriate tempo.

It is well known that Hesse, in accordance with the Bach tradition that had come down to him, used to play the organ compositions in a calm rhythm. If the wonderful vigor of the Bach line of melody is properly brought out by perfect phrasing, the listener does not perceive it as slow, even if it does not go beyond the speed of a moderato.

Since it is impossible to accent individual notes on the organ, the phrasing must be worked out without any support from that kind of accentuation. A plastic rendering of Bach on the organ therefore means giving listeners the illusion of accents through perfect phrasing. It is because this is not yet recognized as the first requirement for all organ playing and the playing of Bach in particular that one so seldom hears Bach's compositions rendered satisfactorily. And how perfectly lucid must the playing be when it has to triumph over the acoustical hazards of a large church!

For those who were acquainted solely with the modern organ, Widor and I therefore proposed an appropriate rendering of Bach's organ compositions that would be new to them and in contrast to the modern, showy style with which they were familiar. We pointed out again and again how difficult it was to play Bach on the modern organ. We expected that the demands the works of Bach make on the organ would do more to popularize the ideal of the real, fine-toned organ than any number of essays on organ building and the techniques required for the performance of Bach. We have not been disappointed.

We could only complete the first five volumes of the new edition containing the sonatas, the concertos, the preludes, and the fugues before my departure for Africa. We intended to complete the three volumes containing the choral preludes during my first leave in Europe, based on drafts I would make in Africa.

At the publisher's request our work was published in three languages. The differences between the French text, on the one hand, and the German together with the English, which is based on it, on the other, reflect the differences of our conventions. Widor and I agreed that in the French edition, his advice, which corresponded to the characteristics of the French organs, should prevail, while in the German and the English, mine should dominate as they reflected the character of the modern organ predominant in those countries.

Soon afterward World War I broke out and communication among publishers of different nations was interrupted. For this reason the edition was published in New York and is primarily distributed in English-speaking countries. In France and Germany the price is prohibitive.

First Activities in Africa, 1913–1917

13

On the afternoon of Good Friday, 1913, my wife and I left Günsbach; on the evening of March 26 we embarked at Bordeaux. At Lambaréné the missionaries gave us a very hearty welcome.

Unfortunately, they had not been able to erect the little buildings of corrugated iron in which I was to begin my medical practice, for they had not secured the necessary laborers. The trade in okoume wood, which was just beginning to flourish in the Ogowe district, offered any able African better-paid work than he could find on the mission station. So at first I had to use an old chicken coop near our living quarters as my consulting room.

By late autumn I was able to move to a corrugated-iron building twenty-six feet long and thirteen feet wide, with a roof of palm leaves, down by the river. It contained a small consulting room, an operating room of similar proportions, and a still-smaller dispensary. Around this building a number of large bamboo huts were gradually constructed for the African patients. The white patients found quarters in the mission house and in the doctor's little bungalow.

From the very first days, even before I had found time to unpack my drugs and instruments, I was besieged by sick people. The choice of Lambaréné as the site of the hospital was based on its geographic location and on the information given us by Mr. Morel, the missionary, a native of Alsace. It proved to be the right decision in every respect. From a distance of one to two hundred miles, upstream or downstream, the sick could be brought to me in canoes along the Ogowe and its tributaries.

The chief diseases I had to deal with were malaria, leprosy, sleeping sickness, dysentery, frambesia, and phagedenic ulcers, but I was surprised by the number of cases of pneumonia and heart disease I discovered. There were also many with urinary tract diseases. Surgical treatment was called for chiefly in cases of hernia and elephantiasis tumors. Hernia is much more common among the native people in equatorial Africa than among white people. If there is no doctor in the region, every year many of the poor people are condemned to a painful death from strangulated hernia, from which a timely operation could have saved them. My first surgical case was of that nature.

Thus during the very first weeks I realized that the physical misery among the Africans was not less but much greater than I had expected. How glad I was that in defiance of all objections, I had carried out my plan of going there as a doctor!

Great was the joy of Dr. Nassau, the aged founder of the mission station at Lambaréné, when I wrote to him in America that the station once more had the services of a physician.

An initial handicap in my work consisted in the difficulty of finding Africans who could serve as interpreters and helpers at the infirmary. The first who proved himself capable of assisting was a former cook by the name of Joseph Azoawani. He stayed with me, though I could not pay him as much as he had earned in his former job. He gave me some valuable hints about how to deal with the Africans, though I was unable to agree with the one he thought most important. He advised me to reject patients whose lives, so far as we could see, could not be saved. Again and again he held up to me the example of the fetishistic doctors who would have nothing to do with such cases so as to endanger as little as possible their reputation as healers.

But on one point I later had to admit that he was right. When dealing with Africans, one must never hold out hope of recovery to the patient and his relatives if the case is really hopeless. If death occurs without warning, they conclude that the doctor did not know that the disease would have this outcome because he had not diagnosed it correctly. One must tell the truth to African patients without reservation. They wish to know it, and they can bear it. Death for them is something natural. They are not afraid of it, but, on the contrary, face it calmly. If, against all expectations, the patient recovers, the doctor's reputation increases immensely. He is seen as one who can cure even fatal diseases.

My wife, who had been trained as a nurse, gave me invaluable assistance at the hospital. She looked after the serious cases, oversaw the laundry and the bandages, worked in the dispensary, sterilized the surgical instruments, made all the preparations for the operations herself, and administered the anesthetics, while Joseph acted as assistant. That she managed the complicated African household successfully and still could find some hours to spare for the hospital every day was really an amazing achievement.

To persuade the Africans that they needed an operation required no great skill from me. A few years earlier a government physician, Dr. Jauré Guibert, had performed several successful operations when he stayed at Lambaréné on one of his journeys, so nobody had reason to be afraid of my modest surgical skills. Fortunately I did not lose a single one of the first patients on whom I operated.

After a few months the hospital had to accommodate about forty patients every day. I had, however, to provide shelter not only for these but for their companions, who had brought them long distances in canoes and who stayed to paddle them back home again.

Heavy as it was, I found the actual work a lighter burden than the care and responsibility that came with it. Unfortunately I am among those doctors who do not have the robust temperament desirable for this calling, but who worry about the condition of the seriously ill and of those who have undergone an operation. In vain have I tried to achieve that equanimity that permits the doctor to combine compassion for his patients with the necessary preservation of his own energies.

Insofar as the rule could be enforced, I used to exact from my African patients some tangible evidence of their appreciation for the help they had received. Again and again I used to remind them that they enjoyed the blessing of the hospital because so many people in Europe had made sacrifices to provide it; it was, therefore, now their duty to give all the help they could to keep it going. Thus I gradually developed the practice whereby, in return for the medicines given, I would receive gifts of money, bananas, poultry, or eggs. These did not, of course, approach the value of the medicines, but it was a modest contribution to the upkeep of the hospital. With the bananas I could feed the sick whose provisions had given out, and with the money I could buy rice if the supply of bananas failed. I also thought that the Africans would appreciate the value of the hospital more if they themselves contributed to its maintenance, according to their ability, than if they simply got everything for nothing.

Experience has confirmed the educational value of some form of payment. Of course no gift was exacted from the very poor and the old—and among the Africans age always means poverty. The most primitive among them, however, had a different conception of this present. When they left the hospital cured, they demanded a gift from me because I had now become their friend.

In my exchanges with these primitive people I naturally asked myself the much debated question of whether they were mere prisoners of tradition, or whether they were capable of independent thought. In the conversations I had with them I found to my surprise that they were far more interested in the elemental questions about the meaning of life and the nature of good and evil than I had supposed.

As I had expected, the questions of dogma to which the Missionary Society's committee in Paris had attached so much importance played practically no part in the sermons of the missionaries. If they wanted to be understood by their listeners they could do nothing beyond preaching the simple Gospel of becoming freed from the world by the spirit of Jesus, the Gospel that comes to us in the Sermon on the Mount and the finest sayings of Paul.

Necessity compelled them to present Christianity primarily as an ethical religion. When they met twice a year for conferences at different mission stations, they focused on the practical application of the Gospels, and not on problems of dogma. That some were more strict about matters of doctrine than others did not influence their missionary work, which they shared. As I did not make the smallest attempt to disturb them with my theological views, they soon laid aside all mistrust and rejoiced, as I did, that we were united in the piety of obedience to Jesus and in the will to simple Christian activity. Not many months after my arrival, they asked me to preach, and thus I was released from the promise I had given in Paris *d'être muet comme une carpe*.

I was also invited to attend as an observer the meetings of the Synod when the missionaries and the African preachers sat in council together. One day, when I had expressed my opinion on a certain point at the request of the missionaries, one of the African preachers suggested that the matter was outside the Doctor's province "because he is not a theologian."

I was also allowed to participate in the examination of the candidates for baptism. I generally got them to send me one or two old women so that I could make the trying half hour as easy as possible for them. On one such occasion, when I put to one worthy matron the question of whether the Lord Jesus had been rich or poor, she replied: "What a stupid question! If God, the Great Chief, was His Father, He certainly can't have been poor." And in general she answered with the Canaanite woman's quickness of repartee. It was, however, of no help to her that the professor of theology gave her a good grade. The African preacher to whose district she belonged dealt with her more strictly so as to punish her for not having attended the catechism classes regularly. Her excellent answers found no favor in his eyes; he wanted to hear those that were in the catechism. So she failed and had to take the examination again six months later.

I found preaching a great joy. To be allowed to preach the sayings of Jesus and Paul to people for whom they were quite new was a wonderful experience. As interpreters I had the African teachers of the mission school, who translated each sentence at once into the language of the Galoas or of the Pàhouins, or sometimes into both in succession.

The little spare time that was at my disposal in the first year at Lambaréné I devoted to work on the last three volumes of the American edition of Bach's organ music.

For keeping up my organ playing I had the magnificent piano with pedal attachment, built specially for the tropics, which the Paris Bach Society had presented to me in recognition of my many years of service as their organist.

At first, however, I lacked the courage to practice. I had tried to get used to the thought that my work in Africa would mean the end of my life as an artist and that renunciation of it would be easier if I allowed fingers and feet to grow rusty. One evening, however, as, in a melancholy mood, I was playing one of Bach's organ fugues, it suddenly occurred to me that I might after all use my free hours in Africa to improve my technique and interpretation. I immediately decided to select compositions of Bach, Mendelssohn, Widor, César Franck, and Max Reger, and to study them carefully down to the smallest detail, learning them by heart, even if a single piece took weeks or months.

How I enjoyed being able to practice in my spare time, quietly and without being harassed by concert schedules, even though sometimes I could find only a half hour in the day.

My wife and I had now completed our second dry season in Africa and were making plans for a trip home at the beginning of the third when, on August 5, 1914, the news came that war had broken out in Europe.

On the evening of that very day we were informed that we must consider ourselves prisoners of war; we might remain in our own house for the present, but we must cease all contact with either white people or Africans and obey unconditionally the orders of the African soldiers who were assigned to be our guards. One of the missionaries and his wife, who like ourselves were Alsatians, were also interned at the Lambaréné mission station.

At first the Africans experienced only one aspect of the war: the timber trade was interrupted, and all commodities had become more expensive. Only later, when many of them were transported to Cameroon to serve as carriers for the active forces, did they understand what the war really meant.

When it became known that, of the white men who used to live on the Ogowe, ten had already been killed, an old African remarked: "What, so many men killed already in this war! Why don't their tribes talk it out in a palaver? How can they ever pay for all these dead men?" For in African warfare those who die, whether among the conquerors or the conquered, have to be paid for by the opposite side. This same man observed that Europeans kill each other merely out of cruelty, and not out of necessity, because they don't eat the dead.

That white people were making prisoners of other whites and putting them under the authority of black soldiers was something incomprehensible to the Africans. What a torrent of abuse my African guards came in for from the people of the neighboring villages because they thought the guards were "the Doctor's masters."

When I was forbidden to work in the hospital, I thought at first that I would proceed with the completion of my book on Paul. But at once another subject forced itself upon me, one about which I had thought for many years and which became a timely issue because of the war: the problem of our civilization. So on the second day of my internment, still quite amazed at being able to sit down at my writing table early in the morning as in the days before I took up medicine, I set to work on *The Philosophy of Civilization*.

The idea of pursuing this subject had first come to me in the summer of 1899 at the house of Ernst Curtius in

Berlin. Hermann Grimm and others were conversing there one evening about a session of the academy from which they had just come when suddenly one of them—I forget who it was—exclaimed, "So we are all nothing but epigones!" This pronouncement struck me like a bolt of lightning, because it put into words what I myself felt.

Since my first years at the university I had grown to doubt increasingly the idea that mankind is steadily moving toward improvement. My impression was that the fire of its ideals was burning out without anyone noticing or worrying about it. On a number of occasions I had seen public opinion failing to reject officially proclaimed theses that were barbaric; on the contrary, it approved inhumane conduct whether by governments or individuals. What was just and equitable seemed to be pursued with only lukewarm zeal. I noticed a number of symptoms of intellectual and spiritual fatigue in this generation that is so proud of its achievements. It seemed as if I were hearing its members trying to convince one another that their previous hopes for the future of mankind had been placed too high, and that it was becoming necessary to limit oneself to striving for what was attainable. The slogan of the day, "Realpolitik," meant approval of a shortsighted nationalism and a pact with the forces and tendencies that had hitherto been resisted as enemies of progress. One of the most visible signs of decline seemed to be the return of superstition, long banished from the educated circles of society.

Toward the end of the nineteenth century, when people began to review their past achievements in order to measure the progress that had been made, they displayed an optimism that I found incomprehensible. It was assumed everywhere not only that we had made progress in inventions and knowledge but that in the intellectual and ethical spheres we lived and moved at a height that had never before been attained and should never be lost. My own impression was that in our intellectual and spiritual life not only had we sunk below the level of past generations, but we were in many respects merely living on their achievements, and that not a little of this heritage was beginning to melt away in our hands.

And now, here was someone expressing the criticism that I myself had silently and half unconsciously leveled against our age! After that evening at Professor Curtius's house, along with my other work I always considered writing a book with the title "Wir Epigonen" (We Inheritors of a Past).

When I discussed these thoughts with my friends, they usually took them to be interesting paradoxes and manifestations of a fin-de-siècle pessimism. After that, I kept my ideas strictly to myself. Only in my sermons did I express my doubts concerning our culture and spirituality.

Now war had broken out as a result of the collapse of our civilization. "We Inheritors of a Past," then, had lost its meaning. The book had been conceived as a criticism of civilization. It was meant to demonstrate its decadence and to draw attention to its inherent dangers. But since the catastrophe had already come about, what good could come of deliberating about the causes?

I thought of writing for my own sake this book, which had thus become out of date. But could I be certain that the manuscript would not be taken from a prisoner of war? Was there any prospect of my returning to Europe again? In this spirit of complete detachment I set to work and went on with it even after I was allowed to go about and devote myself to the sick again.

Albert Schweitzer (in the second row, with the white collar) with his classmates in Günsbach, when he was about seven years old. *Courtesy of
Gustav Woytt*

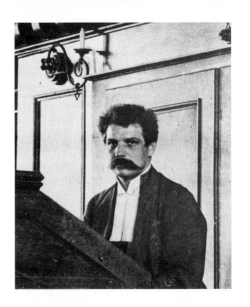

At the organ, about 1898. *Courtesy of the Albert Schweitzer Archives, Günsbach*

Schweitzer (first row, center) with the students of the Collegium Wilhelmitanum at Strasbourg, 1902. *Courtesy of Gustav Woytt*

With his wife, Helene, in Colmar, 1912 (the year of their wedding and one year before they departed for Lambaréné). *Courtesy of Gustav Woytt*

On the hillside near the Ogowe River, the site of his first hospital, during his first period at Lambaréné, 1913–1917. *Courtesy of Gustav Woytt*

As prisoner of war at St. Rémy de Provence in France, 1918. *Courtesy of Gustav Woytt*

Schweitzer with Pablo Casals, in Zürich in 1953, when Casals pleaded with Schweitzer to speak out on nuclear issues. © *Erica Anderson, Albert Schweitzer Center, Great Barrington, Massachusetts*

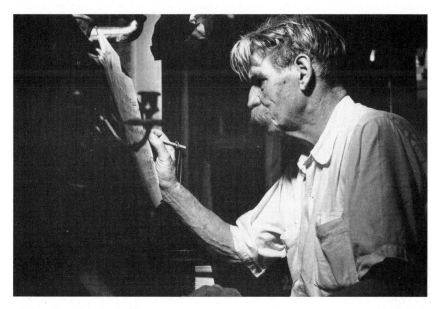

Above: Schweitzer at his piano, sent to Lambaréné as a gift by the Paris Bach Society, 1950s. © *Erica Anderson, Albert Schweitzer Center, Great Barrington, Massachusetts. Below:* With a Gabonese patient, around 1957. © *Erica Anderson, Albert Schweitzer Center, Great Barrington, Massachusetts*

Sunday sermon at Lambaréné: Schweitzer with two Gabonese interpreters, 1950s. *Courtesy of Gustav Woytt*

With leper children at their French lesson in Lambaréné, around 1960. © *Erica Anderson, Albert Schweitzer Center, Great Barrington, Massachusetts*

Schweitzer, in 1959, studying a Bach score at Tübingen, where the manuscript for the edition of the last volumes of the complete organ works was stored during World War II. © *Erica Anderson, Albert Schweitzer Center, Great Barrington, Massachusetts*

At the end of November, thanks to Widor's intervention, as I learned afterward, we were released from our internment. Even before that the order that kept me away from the sick had proved impossible to enforce. White and black alike had protested against being deprived of the services of the only doctor for hundreds of miles around for no apparent reason. The district commandant therefore felt obliged to give now to one, now to another, a note for my guards, telling them to let the bearer pass because he needed my help.

After I resumed my medical activities in relative freedom, I still found time to work on the book on civilization. Many a night I sat thinking and writing, overcome with emotion as I thought of those who at that very hour were lying in the trenches.

At the beginning of the summer of 1915 I awoke from some kind of mental daze. Why only criticize civilization? Why limit myself to analyzing ourselves as *epigones*? Why not work on something constructive?

I then began to search for the knowledge and convictions that comprise the will to civilization and the power to realize it. "We Inheritors of a Past" expanded into a work dealing with the restoration of civilization.

As I worked along, the connection between civilization and our concept of the world became clear to me. I recognized that the catastrophe of civilization stemmed from a catastrophe in our thinking.

The ideals of true civilization had lost their power because the idealistic attitude toward life in which they are rooted had gradually been lost. All the events that occur within nations and within mankind can be traced to spiritual causes stemming from the prevailing attitude toward life.

But what is civilization?

The essential element in civilization is the ethical perfecting of the individual as well as society. At the same time, every spiritual and every material step forward has significance for civilization. The will to civilization is, then, the universal will to progress that is conscious of the ethical as the highest value. In spite of the great importance we attach to the achievements of science and human prowess, it is obvious that only a humanity that is striving for ethical ends can benefit in full measure from material progress and can overcome the dangers that accompany it. The present situation was terrible proof of the misjudgment of the generation that had adopted a belief in an immanent power of progress realizing itself, naturally and automatically, and which thought that it no longer needed any ethical ideals but could advance toward its goals by means of knowledge and work alone.

The only possible way out of chaos is for us to adopt a concept of the world based on the ideals of true civilization.

But what is the nature of that concept of the world in which the will to general progress and the will to ethical progress join and are linked together?

It consists in an ethical affirmation of the world and of life.

What is affirmation of the world and of life?

To us Europeans and to people of European descent everywhere, the will to progress is something so natural and so much a matter of course that it never occurs to us that it is rooted in a concept of life and springs from an act of the spirit. But if we look around us, we soon notice that what we take for granted is not at all natural everywhere.

In Indian thought all efforts to acquire knowledge and power and to improve the living conditions of man and society as a whole are considered mere folly. It teaches that the only wise attitude for a person is to withdraw entirely into himself and to concern himself with the perfecting of his inner life. What may become of human society and of mankind does not concern the individual. The meditation on the inner life in Indian thought consists of man's submission to the idea of giving up his will to live; it reduces his earthly existence to abstinence from all action and to negation of life in order to achieve a state of nonbeing.

It is interesting to trace the origin of this unnatural idea of negation of the world. At first it had nothing whatever to do with any concept of the world, but was a magical idea of the Brahmin priests of early times. They believed that by detachment from the world and from life they could become supernatural beings and obtain magical powers. The experience of ecstasy has contributed to the growth of this idea.

In the course of time this rejection of the world and of life, which was originally the privilege of the Brahmin, was developed into a system of thought that claimed to be valid for all men.

Whether the will to progress is present or not depends, then, on the prevailing concept of the world and of life. A concept that negates this world excludes progress, while affirmation demands it. Among primitive and semiprimitive peoples, who have not yet faced the problem of acceptance or rejection of the world, there is also no will to progress. Their ideal is the simplest life with the least possible trouble.

We Europeans have only arrived at our will to progress in the course of time and through a change in our conception of the world. In antiquity and in the Middle Ages we can find the first attempts. Greek thinking does try to establish an affirmative attitude toward the world and toward life, but it fails in the attempt and ends in resignation. The attitude of the Middle Ages is determined by the ideas of primitive Christianity brought into harmony with Greek metaphysics. It is fundamentally a rejection of the world and of life because Christianity focused on the world beyond, rather than on life on this earth. What manifests itself as affirmation of the world in the Middle Ages is inspired by the active ethic contained in the preaching of Jesus, and it is made possible through the creative forces of fresh and unspoiled peoples on whom Christianity had imposed a concept of the world that was in contradiction to their nature.

Gradually, the affirmation of life, already latent among the European peoples as a result of the Great Migration, begins to manifest itself. The Renaissance proclaims its freedom from the medieval negation of the world and of life. An ethical character is given to this new world-accepting attitude by incorporating the ethic of love taught by Jesus. This, as an ethic of action, is strong enough to reject the negative concept of the world from which it had issued, and to arrive at the new affirmative attitude toward the world and life. In this way it attained the ideal realization of a spiritual and ethical world within the natural.

The striving for material and spiritual progress that characterizes the people of modern Europe, therefore, has its source in the worldview at which these people had arrived.

As heir to the Renaissance and the spiritual and religious movements connected with it, man gains a new perspective of himself and of the world. A need awakens to create spiritual and material values that would bring about change in individuals and in mankind. The modern European is not only enthusiastic about progress to his personal advantage. He is less concerned about his own fate than about the happiness of future generations. Enthusiasm for progress has taken possession of him. Impressed by his discovery that the world is created and sustained by forces according to a definite design, he wills himself to become the active, purposeful force in the world. He looks with confidence toward the new and better times that will dawn for mankind. He learns by experience that ideas held and acted upon by the masses can gain power over circumstances and transform them.

It is upon this will to material progress, acting in conjunction with the will to ethical progress, that modern civilization is founded.

There is an essential relationship between the modern European attitude of ethical affirmation toward the world and life and that of Zarathustra and of Chinese thought, as we encounter it in the writings of Cong-tse, Meng-tse, Mitse, and the other great ethical thinkers of China.

In each of these we can see the striving to remold the circumstances of peoples and of makind to achieve progress, even if the efforts are not as strong as those of modern Europe. In areas under the religious influences of Zarathustra and the Chinese, a life-affirming civilization actually emerged. But they both met with a tragic end. The neo-

Persian civilization based on the philosophy of Zarathustra was destroyed by Islam. The Chinese civilization is hampered in its natural development and threatened with decay by the pressure exerted upon it by European ideas and problems and by confusion caused by the country's political and economic disorder.

In modern European thought the tragedy is that the original bonds uniting the affirmative attitude toward the world with ethics are, by a slow but irresistible process, loosening and finally breaking apart. They will end in disintegration. European humanity is being guided by a will to progress that has become merely external and has lost its bearings.

By itself the affirmation of life can only produce a partial and imperfect civilization. Only if it turns inward and becomes ethical can the will to progress attain the ability to distinguish the valuable from the worthless. We must therefore strive for a civilization that is not based on the accretion of science and power alone, but which cares most of all for the spiritual and ethical development of the individual and of humankind.

How could it come about that the modern concept of the world and of life changed its original ethical character to a nonethical one?

The only possible explanation is that the ethical was not really founded on thought. The thought out of which it arose was noble and enthusiastic but not deep. The intimate connection between the ethical and the affirmative attitude toward life was a matter of intuition and experience, but was not based on proof. It proclaimed the affirmation of life and ethical principles without having penetrated to their essence and their inner connection.

This noble and valuable concept of the world was based on belief in, rather than consistent thought about, the real nature of things; thus it was destined to fade with time and to lose its power over man's mind.

All subsequent thinking about the problems of ethics and man's relation to his world could not but expose the weak points of this view. Thus, in spite of the original intention to defend this concept, it hastened its demise. It never succeeded in replacing an inadequate with an adequate foundation. Again and again attempts to build new foundations proved too weak to support the superstructure.

With my apparently abstract yet absolutely practical thinking about the connection of civilization with philosophy, I had come to see the decay of civilization as a consequence of the continuous weakening of the ethical affirmation of life within modern worldviews. It had become clear to me that, like so many other people, I had clung to that concept of decay from inner necessity, without asking myself to what extent it could be supported by thought.

I had got thus far during the summer of 1915. What was to come next? Could the difficulty be solved that until now had seemed insoluble? Was it imaginable that the worldview that alone had made civilization possible was an illusion destined to stir our minds but always remain hidden? To continue to hold this illusion up to our generation seemed to me absurd and degrading. Only if it offers itself to us as something arising from thought can it become our own spiritually.

Fundamentally I remained convinced that ethics and the affirmation of life are interdependent and the precondition for all true civilization. A first step out of this impasse seemed imperative: to attain, through new, sincere, and direct contemplation, that truth we have hoped for in the past and which sometimes even seemed to be real.

In undertaking this I felt like someone who has to replace a rotten boat that is no longer seaworthy with a new and better one, but does not know how to proceed.

For months on end I lived in a continual state of mental agitation. Without the least success I concentrated—even during my daily work at the hospital—on the real nature of the affirmation of life and of ethics and on the question of what they have in common. I was wandering about in a thicket where no path was to be found. I was pushing against an iron door that would not yield.

All that I had learned from philosophy about ethics left me dangling in midair. The notions of the Good that it had offered were all so lifeless, so unelemental, so narrow, and so lacking in content that it was impossible to relate them to an affirmative attitude.

Moreover, philosophy never, or only rarely, concerned itself with the problem of the connection between civilization and concepts of the worldview. The affirmation of life in modern times seemed so natural that no need was felt to explore its meaning.

To my surprise I recognized that the central province of philosophy into which my reflections on civilization and the worldview had led me was virtually unexplored territory. Now from this point, now from that, I tried to penetrate to its interior, but again and again I had to give up the attempt. I saw before me the concept that I wanted, but I could not catch hold of it. I could not formulate it.

While in this mental state I had to take a long journey on the river. I was staying with my wife on the coast at

Cape Lopez for the sake of her health—it was in September, 1915—when I was called out to visit Madame Pelot, the ailing wife of a missionary, at N'Gômô, about 160 miles upstream. The only transportation I could find was a small steamer, which was about to leave, towing two overloaded barges. In addition to myself, only Africans were on board, among them my friend Emil Ogouma from Lambaréné. Since I had been in too much of a hurry to arrange for enough provisions for the journey, they invited me to share their food.

Slowly we crept upstream, laboriously navigating—it was the dry season—between the sandbanks. Lost in thought I sat on the deck of the barge, struggling to find the elementary and universal concept of the ethical that I had not discovered in any philosophy. I covered sheet after sheet with disconnected sentences merely to concentrate on the problem. Two days passed. Late on the third day, at the very moment when, at sunset, we were making our way through a herd of hippopotamuses, there flashed upon my mind, unforeseen and unsought, the phrase "reverence for life." The iron door had yielded. The path in the thicket had become visible. Now I had found my way to the principle in which affirmation of the world and ethics are joined together!

I was at the root of the problem. I knew that the ethical acceptance of the world and of life, together with the ideals of civilization contained in this concept, has its foundation in thought.

What is Reverence for Life, and how does it develop in us?

If man wishes to have a clear idea about himself and his relation to the world, he must turn away from the various concepts created by his reason and knowledge and reflect upon his own consciousness, the elemental, the most immediate reality. Only if he starts from this given fact can he arrive at a thoughtful concept.

Descartes begins with the sentence "I think, therefore I am" (*Cogito, ergo sum*). With his beginning thus chosen, he pursues the road to the abstract. Out of this act of thinking, which is without substance and artificial, nothing concerning the relation of man to himself and to the universe can come. In reality, however, the most immediate act of consciousness has some content. To think means to think something. The most immediate fact of man's consciousness is the assertion "I am life that wills to live in the midst of life that wills to live," and it is as will to live in the midst of will to live that man conceives himself at every moment that he spends meditating on himself and the world around him.

As my will to live includes an ardent desire to perpetuate life and the mysterious exaltation of the will to live, which we call happiness, and while there is fear of destruction and of the mysterious damage of the will to live, which we call pain, so too is this will to live in those around me, whether it expresses itself to me or remains mute.

Man must now decide how he will live in the face of his will to live. He can deny it. But if he wants to change his will to live into the will not to live, as is the case in Indian and indeed in all pessimistic thought, he creates a contradiction with himself. He builds his philosophy of life on a false premise, something that cannot be realized.

Indian thought, like that of Schopenhauer, is full of contradictions because it cannot help but make concessions over and over again to the will to live, which persists in spite of all negation of the world, though it will not admit that these are concessions. Negation of the will to live is only consistent with itself if it decides to put an end to physical existence.

If man affirms his will to live, he acts naturally and sincerely. He confirms an act, which has already been accomplished unconsciously, by bringing it to his conscious thought.

The beginning of thought, a beginning that continually repeats itself, is that man does not simply accept his existence as something given, but experiences it as something unfathomably mysterious.

Affirmation of life is the spiritual act by which man ceases to live thoughtlessly and begins to devote himself to his life with reverence in order to give it true value. To affirm life is to deepen, to make more inward, and to exalt the will to live.

At the same time the man who has become a thinking being feels a compulsion to give to every will to live the same reverence for life that he gives to his own. He experiences that other life in his own. He accepts as good preserving life, promoting life, developing all life that is capable of development to its highest possible value. He considers as evil destroying life, injuring life, repressing life that is capable of development. This is the absolute, fundamental principle of ethics, and it is a fundamental postulate of thought.

Until now the great weakness in all ethical systems has been that they dealt only with the relations of man to man. In reality, however, the question is, What is our attitude toward the universe and all that it supports? A man is ethical only when life as such is sacred to him—the life of plants and animals as well as that of his fellow men—and when he devotes himself to helping all life that is in need of help.

Only the universal ethic of growing responsibility for all that lives—only that ethic can be founded solidly in thought. The ethic of the relation of man to man is nothing but a fragment of the universal ethic.

The ethic of Reverence for Life, therefore, comprehends within itself everything that can be described as love, devotion, and compassion in suffering, the sharing of joy and common endeavors.

The world, however, offers us the horrible drama of will to live divided against itself. One existence holds its own at the cost of another; one destroys another. Only in the thinking man has the will to live become conscious of other wills to live and desirous of solidarity with them. This solidarity, however, he cannot completely bring about, because man is subject to the puzzling and horrible law of being obliged to live at the cost of other life and to incur again and again the guilt of destroying and injuring life. But as an ethical being he strives to escape whenever possible from this necessity, and as one who has become knowing and merciful, he tries to end this division of the will to live insofar as it is in his power. He aspires to prove his humanity and to release others from their sufferings.

Reverence for Life arising from the will to live that is inspired by thought contains the affirmation of life and ethics inseparably combined. It seeks to create values and to make progress of various kinds that will serve the material, spiritual, and ethical development of the individual and of mankind.

While the unthinking modern affirmation of life vacillates between its ideals of science and those of power, a reflective affirmation of life proposes the spiritual and ethical perfecting of mankind as the highest ideal, an ideal from which alone all other ideals of progress receive their real value.

Through ethical affirmation of the world and of life, we reach a deeper comprehension of life that enables us to distinguish between what is essential in civilization and what is not. The absurd pretension of considering ourselves civilized loses its power over us. We confront the truth that, with so much progress in knowledge and power, it has become not easier but more difficult to attain true civilization.

The problem of the mutual relationship between the spiritual and the material dawns on us. We know that we all have to struggle with circumstances to preserve our own humanity. We must do all we can so that the desperate struggle that many fight in order to preserve their humanity amid unfavorable social circumstances will become a battle that has a chance of success.

A deepened ethical will to progress that springs from thought will lead us back, then, out of our poor civilization with its many faults to true civilization. Sooner or later the true and final renaissance must dawn, which will bring peace to the world.

By then a plan for my whole *Philosophy of Civilization* stood our clearly in my mind. It fell quite naturally into four parts: (1) the present lack of civilization and its causes; (2) a discussion of the idea of Reverence for Life in relation to the attempts made in the past by European philosophy to provide a foundation for an affirmative ethical attitude toward the world; (3) an exposition of the concept of Reverence for Life; (4) the civilized state.

The writing of the second part, the description of European philosophy's tragic struggle to arrive at an ethical basis for acceptance of the world, was forced upon me. I felt an inner need to explore the historical development of the problem and to offer my solution as a synthesis of all previous solutions. I have never regretted having succumbed to this temptation. In my attempt to understand the thought of others my own became clearer.

I had brought some of the philosophical works needed for this historical research with me to Africa. The others I needed were sent to me by Mr. Strohl, professor of zoology at Zürich, and his wife. The well-known Bach singer, Robert Kaufmann of Zürich, whom I had so often accompanied on the organ, also helped to keep me in touch with the outside world, with the assistance of the Office des Internés Civils at Geneva.

Without haste I sketched rough drafts of the material I had collected and sifted, without regard to the structure of the final treatise. At the same time I began to write out individual sections.

Every day I was aware of the great blessing that I could save lives while others were forced to kill, and that at the same time I could work toward the coming of the era of peace.

Fortunately my supply of drugs and bandages did not give out, for I had received a large supply of all necessary items from one of the last boats to arrive before the outbreak of war.

Because my wife's health had suffered from the stifling air of Lambaréné, we spent the rainy season of 1916–1917 on the coast. A timber merchant provided us with a house at Chienga near Cape Lopez at the mouth of one of the tributaries of the Ogowe. It was the home of an employee of his who had looked after the timber rafts, but as a consequence of the war it now stood empty. In return for his kindness I joined his African workers rolling the okoume logs, which had already been tied together in rafts, onto dry land. They then would be preserved from ship-worms during the long interval that might elapse before cargoes could again be shipped to Europe.

This heavy work—we often needed hours to roll up on the shore a single log weighing from two to three tons—was possible only at high tide. When the tide was low, I sat with my *Philosophy of Civilization*, insofar as my time was not claimed by patients.

Garaison and St. Rémy

14

In September 1917, just after I had resumed my work in Labaréné, we received orders to embark at once on the next ship to Europe, to be placed in a prisoner-of-war camp. Fortunately the ship was a few days late, so with the help of the missionaries and a few Africans, we had time to pack our belongings, including drugs and instruments, in cases and to stow them all in a small corrugated-iron building.

It would have been useless to consider taking the sketches for *The Philosophy of Civilization* with me. They might have been confiscated at any customs inspection. I therefore entrusted them to the American missionary, Mr. Ford, who was then working at Lambaréné. He admitted to me that he would have preferred to throw the heavy packet into the river, because he considered philosophy to be unnecessary and harmful. However, out of Christian charity he was willing to keep it and send it to me at the end of the war. To save what I had already done in the event that something might happen to it, I spent two nights writing a summary in French that contained the main ideas and the sequence of the chapters already finished. So that it would appear remote from actual life and therefore inoffensive to the censors, I inserted chapter headings to make it look like a historical study of the Renaissance. As it turned out, I did in this way secure its escape from confiscation, which on several occasions threatened it.

Two days before our departure, amid packed and half-packed cases, I had to operate with all haste on a strangulated hernia.

Just when we had been taken on board the river steamer and the Africans were shouting to us an affectionate farewell from the bank, the father superior of the Catholic mission came onboard, waved aside with an authoritative gesture the African soldiers who tried to prevent his approach, and shook hands with us. "You shall not leave this country," he said, "without my thanking you both for all the good that you have done." We were never to see each other again. Shortly after the war he lost his life on board the *Afrique*, the ship that had taken us to Europe, when she was wrecked in the Bay of Biscay.

At Cape Lopez a white man whose wife I had once treated as a patient came up to me and offered me some money in case I had none. How grateful I now was for the gold I had taken with me on the chance that war might break out! An hour before we started I had visited an English timber merchant whom I knew well, and had exchanged it at a favorable rate for French notes, which my wife and I now carried sewn into our clothing.

On the liner we were put in charge of a white officer who was obliged to see to it that we had no exchanges with anyone except the steward specifically assigned to us, who at certain appointed hours took us on deck. Since writing was impossible, I filled my time with learning by heart some of Bach's fugues and Widor's Sixth Organ Symphony.

Our steward—whose name, if I remember correctly, was Gaillard—was very good to us. Toward the end of the voyage he asked us whether we had noticed that he had treated us with special kindness considering that we were prisoners. "I always served your meals promptly, and your cabin was just as clean as that of the others." (This was an accurate statement in view of the untidiness of the African ships during the war.) "Can you guess," he continued, "why I did this? Certainly not because I expected a good tip. One never expects that from prisoners. Why then? I'll tell you. A few months ago a Mr. Gaucher, whom you had had as a patient for months in your hospital, traveled home in this ship in one of my cabins. 'Gaillard,' he said to me, 'it may happen that before long you will be taking the Lambaréné doctor to Europe as a prisoner. If he ever does travel on your ship, and should you be able to help him in any way, do so for my sake.' Now you know why I took such good care of you."

For three weeks we were put in the *caserne de passage* (temporary barracks) in the rue de Belleville at Bordeaux, where during the war interned foreigners were housed. There I soon developed the symptoms of dysentery. Fortunately I had in my baggage some emetine with which to fight it. I suffered from this illness for a long time afterward, however.

Next we were taken to the huge internment camp at Garaison in the Pyrenees. We mistakenly failed to interpret the order to make ourselves ready for departure during the night as meaning that very night, so we had packed nothing when around midnight two gendarmes came with a carriage to take us away. They were angry at what they supposed to be our disobedience, and since packing by the light of one miserable candle was a very slow process, they became impatient and wanted to take us off, leaving our baggage behind. Finally, however, they had pity on us and even helped us to collect our possessions and to stuff them into our trunks. The memory of those two gendarmes has often since then made me behave patiently with others when impatience seemed justifiable!

When we were deposited at Garaison and the officer on guard was inspecting our baggage, he stumbled onto a French translation of the *Politics* of Aristotle, which I had brought with me with a view to the work on *The Philosophy of Civilization.* "Why, it's incredible!" he stormed. "They're actually bringing political books into a prisoner-of-war camp!" I timidly remarked to him that the book was written long before the birth of Christ. "Hey, scholar, is that true?" he asked of a soldier who was standing nearby. The latter corroborated my statement. "What! You mean to say that people talked politics as long ago as that?" he asked back. Upon our answering in the affirmative, he gave his decision: "Anyhow, we don't say the same things about it today, and as far as I am concerned you can keep your book."

Garaison (Provençal for *guérison*, "healing") was once a large monastery to which the sick came from long distances on pilgrimages. After the separation of church and state it stood empty and in a state of decay until, at the outbreak of war, hundreds of aliens from enemy countries—men, women, and children—were housed in it. In twelve months it was restored to comparatively good condition by craftsmen who were among the interned. The governor of the camp was a retired colonial official named Vecchi, a theosophist, who carried out his duties not only with fairness but with kindness, a fact that was all the more gratefully acknowledged because his predecessor had been strict and harsh.

On the second day after our arrival, as I stood shivering in the courtyard a prisoner introduced himself to me as mill engineer Borkeloh, and asked what he could do to assist me. He was in my debt, he said, because I had cured his wife. That was the case, although I did not know the wife any more than she knew me. It so happened that at the beginning of the war I had given to the representative of a Hamburg timber firm, Richard Classen by name, sent from Lambaréné to a prisoner-of-war camp in Dahomey, a good supply of quinine, Blaud's pills, emetine, arrhenal, bromnatrium, sleeping drafts, and other drugs for himself and the other prisoners whom he would meet. On each bottle I had written detailed directions for use. From Dahomey he was taken to France and found himself in the same camp as Mr. Borkeloh and his wife. When Mrs. Borkeloh lost her appetite and suffered from depression, she was given some of the drugs, which Mr. Classen had as if by a miracle preserved through all the baggage inspections, and she recovered. I now received my fee for this cure

in the form of a table, which Mr. Borkeloh made for me
out of wood he had torn loose somewhere in the loft.
Now I could write . . . and play the organ. On the boat I
had already done some organ practice by using a table as
manual and the floor as pedals, as I had done when I was
a child.

A few days later I was asked by the eldest of some gypsy
musicians who were fellow prisoners whether I was the
Albert Schweitzer whose name occurred in Romain Rolland's book *Musiciens d'aujourd'hui*. When I said yes, he
told me that he and his fellows would regard me from then
on as one of themselves. That meant that I might be present
when they played in the loft and that my wife and I would
be treated to a serenade on our birthdays. In fact my wife
did awake on her birthday to the sounds of the waltz from
The Tales of Hoffmann played with verve and style. These
gypsy performers, who used to play in the fashionable cafés
of Paris, had been allowed to keep their instruments as the
tools of their trade when they were taken prisoner, and
now they were allowed to practice in the camp.

Not long after our arrival some newcomers were brought
from another camp, which had been broken up. They at
once began to grumble about the poorly prepared food and
criticized their fellow prisoners who occupied the much
envied posts in the kitchen as not fit for their job. This
caused great indignation among the latter, who were professional cooks and had come to Garaison from the first-class
hotels and restaurants of Paris!

The matter came before the governor, and when he asked
the rebels which of them were cooks, it turned out that
there was not a single cook among them! Their leader was
a shoemaker, and the others were tailors, hatters, basket

weavers, and brush makers. In their previous camp, however, they had applied themselves to the cooking and declared that they had mastered the art of preparing food in large quantities so that it was just as tasty as when prepared in small quantities. With Solomonic wisdom the governor decided that they should take over the kitchen for a fortnight as an experiment. If they did better than the others, they should keep the posts. Otherwise they would be put under lock and key as disturbers of the peace. On the very first day they proved with potatoes and cabbage that they had not claimed too much, and every succeeding day was a new triumph. So the noncooks were appointed "cooks," and the professional cooks were turned out of the kitchen! When I asked the shoemaker the secret of their success, he replied: "One must know all sorts of things, but most important is to do the cooking with love and care." Now if I learn that someone has been appointed minister of some department in a field about which he knows nothing, I do not get as excited over it as I used to. I keep calm and hope that he will prove as fit for his job as the Garaison shoemaker had proved to be for his.

Strange to say, I was the only physician among the interned. When we arrived, the governor had strictly forbidden me to have anything to do with the sick, since that was the business of the official camp doctor, an old country practitioner from the neighborhood. Later on, however, he thought it only just that I be allowed to let the camp benefit from my professional knowledge, as it did from that of the dentists, of whom there were several among us. He even gave me a room to use for this purpose. As my baggage contained chiefly drugs and instruments, which the sergeant had let me retain after the inspection, I had almost everything that I needed for treatment of the sick. I was able to give especially effective help to those who had been brought there from the colonies, as well as to the many sailors who were suffering from tropical diseases.

Thus I was once more a doctor. What leisure time I had left I devoted to *The Philosophy of Civilization* and to practicing the organ on the table and the floor.

As a physician I got a glimpse of the manifold misery that prevailed in the camp. The worst off were those who suffered mentally from confinement. From the moment we could go down into the courtyard until the trumpet signal that at dusk drove us back, they kept walking round and round looking out over the walls at the glorious white shimmering chain of the Pyrenees. They no longer had the stamina to occupy themselves with anything. When it rained, they stood about apathetically in the passages. In addition, most of them suffered from malnutrition, because they had gradually developed a distaste for the monotonous fare, although it was acceptable for a prisoner-of-war camp. Many suffered from the cold as well, since most of the rooms could not be heated. For these people, weakened in body and soul, the slightest ailment meant a real illness that was very hard to get at and treat successfully. In many cases the depression was prolonged by lamentation over loss of the position they had secured in a foreign land. They did not know where they would go or what they would do when the gates of Garaison opened and let them out. Many had married French women and had children who could speak nothing but French. Could they be asked to leave their homeland? Could they face the struggle of finding acceptance and employment in a new land?

The children of the camp, pale and freezing, and most of them only French-speaking, fought continuous battles in the courtyard and the corridors. Some were for the entente; some were on the side of the central European powers.

To anyone who kept in some measure healthy and vigorous the camp offered much of interest, owing to the fact that people from many nations and of almost every profession were to be found there. There were scholars and artists, especially painters, who had been caught in Paris by the war; German and Austrian shoemakers and dressmakers who had been employed by the big Paris firms; bank directors, hotel managers, waiters, engineers, architects, craftsmen, and businessmen who had made their homes in France and her colonies; Catholic missionaries and members of religious orders from the Sahara, wearing white robes with the red fez; traders from Liberia and other districts on the West Coast of Africa; merchants and commercial travelers from North America, South America, China, and India who had been taken prisoner on the high seas; the crews of German and Austrian merchant ships who had suffered the same fate; Turks, Arabs, Greeks, and nationals of the Balkan States who for various reasons had been deported during the course of operations in the east, and among them Turks with wives who went about veiled. What a motley picture did the courtyard offer twice a day when the roll was called!

No books were needed in the camp to improve one's education. For everything one might want to learn, there were men with specialized knowledge at one's disposal, and from this unique opportunity for learning I profited greatly. About finances, architecture, factory building and equipment, grain growing, furnace building, and many other things, I picked up information I could probably never have acquired elsewhere.

Perhaps the worst sufferers were the craftsmen, condemned to idleness. When my wife secured some material for a warm dress, quite a number of tailors offered to make it for nothing, merely in order to have some cloth in their hands once more, and needle and thread between their fingers.

Permission to help the farmers of the neighborhood in their work was sought not only by those who knew something about agriculture but by many who were accustomed to physical work of any sort. Those who displayed the least desire for activity were the numerous sailors. Their lifestyle onboard ship had taught them how to pass the time together in the simplest ways.

At the beginning of 1918 we were informed that a certain number of the "notables" in the camp would be chosen by last names from each letter of the alphabet and sent to a reprisals camp in North Africa—if I remember rightly—unless by a certain date the measures being taken by the Germans against the civilian population of Belgium were not suspended. We were all advised to send this news home so that our relatives might do whatever necessary to save us from this fate. "Notables," i.e., bank directors, hotel managers, merchants, scholars, artists, and such folk, were chosen because it was assumed that their fate would attract more attention in their home districts than that of the obscure majority. This proclamation brought to light the fact that among our notables were many

persons who were not notable at all. Head waiters, when
delivered here, had given their profession as hotel directors so as to count for something in the camp; shop
assistants had elevated themselves to the rank of merchants. Now they lamented the danger that threatened
them on account of the fictitious ranks they had assumed.
However, all ended well. The measures being taken against
the Belgians were rescinded and Garaison's notables,
whether genuine or fake, had for the present no reprisals
camp to fear.

After a long and severe winter, spring came at last, and
with it an order that my wife and I were to be sent to a
camp intended for Alsatians only, at St. Rémy de Provence. In vain we begged for the rescinding of this order—
the governor, that he might keep his camp doctor, and
we, that we might remain in the camp where we felt at
home.

At the end of March we were transferred to St. Rémy.
The camp was not as cosmopolitan as the one at Garaison.
It was occupied chiefly by teachers, foresters, and railway
employees. But I met there many people I knew, among
them the young Günsbach schoolmaster, John Iltis, and a
young pastor named Liebrich, who had been one of my
students. He had permission to hold services on Sundays
and, as his curate, I was given a good many opportunities
to preach.

The governor, a retired police commissioner from Mar-
seilles named Bagnaud, had established benign rules. Characteristic of his jovial temperament was the answer he used
to give to the question whether such-and-such a thing was

permitted. "Rien n'est permis! Mais il y a des choses qui sont tolérées, si vous vous montrez raisonnables!" ("Nothing is permitted! But there are certain things that are tolerated, if you show yourselves reasonable!") Since he could not pronounce my name he used to call me Monsieur Albert.

The first time I entered the big room on the ground floor where we spent the day it struck me as being strangely familiar in its unadorned and bare ugliness. Where had I seen that iron stove and the flue pipe stretching across the room from one end to another? Eventually the mystery was solved: I knew them from a drawing of van Gogh. The building in which we were housed, once a monastery inside a walled garden, had until recently been occupied by mental patients. Among them at one time had been van Gogh, who immortalized with his pencil the desolate room in which today we in our turn were sitting. Like us, he had suffered from the cold stone floor when the mistral blew! Like us, he had walked round and round behind those high walls!

As one of the interned was a doctor, I had nothing to do with the sick at first, and could spend the whole day with my notes for my philosophy of Western civilization. Later on, my colleague was exchanged and allowed to go home, and I became camp doctor, but the work was not as heavy as at Garaison.

My wife's health had improved considerably in the mountain climate of Garaison, but now she suffered from the harsh winds of Provence. She could not get used to the stone floors. I too felt far from well. Ever since my attack of dysentery at Bordeaux I had been aware of a continually increasing weariness, which I tried in vain to master. I tired easily, and we were both unable to join in the walks the camp inmates were allowed to take on certain days, escorted by the guards. The walks were always at a rapid pace because the prisoners wanted to get as much exercise out of them as possible and to go as far from camp as time permitted. We were thankful indeed that on those days the governor used to take us and other weak prisoners out himself.

Back in Alsace

15

For the sake of my wife, who suffered greatly from confinement and from homesickness, I was glad indeed when, around the middle of July, we were told that we were all, or nearly all, going to be exchanged and should be able to return home via Switzerland in a few days. Fortunately my wife did not notice that my name was missing from the list the governor had been given of those to be released. On July 12, at midnight, we were awakened. An order had been received by telegraph that we should at once make our preparations for departure. This time every name was on the list. As the sun rose we dragged our baggage into the courtyard for inspection. I was allowed to take with me the notes for *The Philosophy of Civilization*, which I had committed to paper here and at Garaison and which had already been checked by the camp censor, after he had put his stamp upon a certain number of pages. As the convoy passed through the gate I ran back to see the governor once more, and found him sitting sorrowfully in his office. He grieved over the departure of his prisoners. We still write to each other, and he addresses me as "mon cher pensionnaire" (my dear boarder).

At the station at Tarascon we had to wait in a distant shed for the arrival of our train. When it came, my wife and I, burdened with heavy luggage, could hardly move. A poor cripple whom I had treated in the camp came forward to help us. He had no baggage because he had no possessions, and I was much moved by his offer, which I accepted. While we walked along side by side in the scorching sun, I vowed to myself that in memory of him I would in future always keep a lookout at stations for heavily laden people and help them. And I have kept this vow. On one occasion, however, my offer made me the suspect of thievish intentions!

Between Tarascon and Lyons we were charmingly received at one station by a committee of ladies and gentlemen and escorted to tables loaded with good food. While we were enjoying ourselves, however, our hosts became curiously embarrassed, and after a few hurried words to each other, they withdrew. They had realized that we were not the guests for whom the welcome and the meal had been intended. They were expecting refugees from occupied territory in northern France, who were being dispatched by the Germans to France through Switzerland after a brief internment, and would now stay for a time in southern France.

When the arrival of a *train d'internés* had been announced, the committee that had been formed to look after these refugees as they passed through took it for granted that we were the travelers they were expecting, and they had only become aware of their mistake when they heard their guests speaking not French but Alsatian. The situation was so comical that it ended with the disillusioned committee joining good-humoredly in the laughter. But best of all most of our party were so busy eating that they noticed nothing since it all happened so quickly, and they journeyed on in the sincere belief that they had done fitting honor to a good meal that had been intended for them.

During the remainder of the journey our train grew longer and longer as the coaches from other camps were added to it one after another at different stations. Two of them were filled with basket and kettle menders, scissors grinders, tramps, and gypsies, who were also being exchanged.

At the Swiss frontier our train was held up for a considerable time until a telegram brought the news that the train conveying the people for whom we were being exchanged had also reached the Swiss frontier.

Early on July 15 we arrived at Zürich. To my astonishment I was called out of the train by Arnold Meyer, the professor of theology, Robert Kaufmann, the singer, and other friends who had gathered to welcome me. They had known for weeks that I was coming.

During the journey to Constance we stood at the windows and could not see enough of the well-cultivated fields and the clean houses of Switzerland. We could hardly grasp the fact that we were in a country that had not been affected by the war.

The impression we received in Constance was dreadful. Here we had before our eyes for the first time the starvation of which until then we had only known by hearsay. Only pale, emaciated people in the streets. How wearily they went about! It was surprising that they could still stand.

My wife received permission to go immediately to Strasbourg with her parents, who had come to meet us. I had to spend another day in Constance with the others and wait until all the necessary formalities were completed. I reached Strasbourg during the night. Not a light was burning in the streets. Not a glimmer of light shining from any dwelling. The city had to be completely dark on account of air attacks. I could not hope to reach the distant garden suburb where my wife's parents lived, and I had considerable trouble finding the way to Frau Fischer's house near St. Thomas.

Since Günsbach was within the sphere of military operations, many office visits and papers were needed to obtain permission to find my father. Trains still ran as far as Colmar, but the ten miles from there toward the Vosges had to be covered on foot.

So this was the peaceful valley that I had left on Good Friday, 1913. There were dull roars from guns in the mountains. On the roads one walked between lines of wire netting packed with straw, as between high walls. These were intended to hide the traffic in the valley from the enemy batteries on the crest of the Vosges.

Everywhere there were concrete emplacements for machine guns. Houses ruined by gunfire. Hills that I had remembered as covered with woods now stood bare. The shell fire had left only a few stumps here and there. In the villages orders were posted that everyone must carry a gas mask with him at all times.

Günsbach was the last inhabited village before the trenches. Hidden by the surrounding mountains, it had not been destroyed by the artillery fire on the heights of the Vosges. Among crowds of soldiers and between lines of battered houses the inhabitants went about their business as if there were no war going on. That they could not bring the second hay crop home from the meadows by day seemed as natural to them as rushing to the cellars whenever the alarm sounded, or the fact that they might at any moment receive an order to evacuate the village on short notice if an attack was imminent, forcing them to leave all their possessions behind.

My father had become so indifferent to danger that he remained in his study during the bombardments, when most people went to their cellars. He could hardly remember a time when he had not shared the vicarage with officers and soldiers.

Anxiety about the harvest, however, weighed heavily on people who had otherwise become indifferent to the war. A terrible drought prevailed. The grain was drying up; the potatoes were ruined; on many meadows the grass crop was so thin that it was not worth mowing; from the stables resounded the bellows of hungry cattle. Even if a storm cloud rose above the horizon it brought not rain but wind, which robbed the soil of its remaining moisture, and clouds of dust adumbrating the specter of starvation.

Meanwhile my wife also had obtained permission to come to Günsbach.

I hoped in vain that among my native hills I should rid myself of the fatigue and the now slight, now severe attacks of the fever from which I had suffered since the last weeks at St. Rémy. From day to day I felt worse until, toward the end of August, a high-fever attack followed by violent pains made me realize that these were the aftereffects of the dysentery I had contracted at Bordeaux and that an immediate operation was necessary. Accompanied by my wife, I dragged myself six kilometers toward Colmar before we could find a vehicle of any sort. On September 1 I was operated on by Professor Stolz in Strasbourg.

As soon as I was able to do some work, the mayor of Strasbourg, Mr. Schwander, offered me a position as a doctor at the municipal hospital, an offer that I joyfully accepted, for I really did not know how I was going to live. I was put in charge of two women's wards in the dermatology department. At the same time I was appointed curate at St. Nicholai once more. I am also deeply indebted to the Chapter of St. Thomas for placing at my disposal the unoccupied parsonage that belonged to the church on the quay of St. Nicholai, although, being only a curate, I had no claim on it.

After the armistice, when Alsace was returned from German rule to French, I was for some time alone in charge of the services at St. Nicholai. Mr. Gerold, who had been removed from his post by the German administration because of his anti-German pronouncements, had not yet been reappointed by the French, and Mr. Ernst, the successor to Mr. Knittel, had been compelled to resign because of his anti-French views.

During the armistice period and the following two years I was a familiar figure to the customs officials at the Rhine Bridge because I frequently went over to Kehl with a knapsack full of provisions for starving friends in Germany. I made a special point of helping in this way Frau Cosima Wagner and the aged painter Hans Thoma, together with his sister Agatha. I had known Hans Thoma for years through Frau Charlotte Schumm, whose late husband had been his childhood friend.

Physician and Preacher in Strasbourg

16

I hoped to spend the little free time my two jobs left me with Bach's choral preludes. As soon as I could reclaim the manuscript I had drafted at Lambaréné, I wanted to finish the last three volumes for the American publisher. But as the parcel seemed never to come and the American publisher showed no desire to rush into publication, I put this work aside and took up *The Philosophy of Civilization*.

While waiting for *The Philosophy of Civilization* manuscript from Africa, I busied myself with studying the great world religions and their conception of the world. As I had examined philosophy in order to see how far it affirms ethical acceptance of the world as a major force in civilization, so now I sought to find out to what extent acceptance and rejection of the world and ethics are contained in Judaism and Christianity, in Islam, in the religion of Zarathustra, in Brahminism, Buddhism, and Hinduism, and in Chinese religious thought.

In this investigation I found full confirmation of my view that civilization is based upon ethical acceptance of the world.

The religions that expressly reject the world and life (Brahminism and Buddhism) show no interest in civilization. While these pessimistic religions leave man to solitary contemplation, the Judaism of the prophetic period, the almost contemporary religion of Zarathustra, and the religious thought of the Chinese contain in their ethical acceptance of the world strong forces that stimulate civilization. They seek to improve social conditions and to call men to purposeful action in the service of common goals that ought to be realized.

The Jewish prophets Amos and Isaiah (760–700 B.C.), Zarathustra (seventh century B.C.), and Cong-tse (560–480 B.C.) mark the great turning point in the spiritual history of mankind. Between the eighth and sixth centuries B.C. thinkers from three nations, living in widely separated countries and having no relations whatever with one another, came at the same time to the conclusion that the ethical consists not in submission to traditional customs, but in the active devotion of the individual to his fellow men or to the improvement of social conditions. In this great revolution begins the spiritual progress of mankind and, with it, the highest potential for the development of civilization.

Christianity and Hinduism are neither completely positive nor negative in their attitude toward the world; both contain the two principles side by side yet in a state of tension with each other. In consequence they can both accept and reject civilization.

Christianity has a negative attitude toward civilization because in the beginning it expected the world to end. For that reason it shows no interest in improving conditions in the natural world. But at the same time, as it contains an active ethic, it vigorously affirms civilization.

In the ancient world, Christianity was a force destructive to civilization. It was partly responsible for the failure of later Stoicism to reform the world and develop ethical human values. The ethical views of the later Stoicism, as we know them from the writings of Epictetus and others, came very near to those of Jesus. The fact remains, however, that Christianity was linked to a negative view of life.

In modern times, under the influence of the Reformation, the Renaissance, and the thinkers of the Enlightenment, Christianity changed its negative attitude toward the world. In primitive Christianity the expectation of the end of the world had not allowed the acceptance of the world. With the affirmation of life, Christianity changed into a religion that could work for, even create, civilization. As such a religion it joined in the struggle against ignorance, want of purpose, cruelty, and injustice, out of which in modern times a new world emerged. Only because the strong ethical energies of Christianity and of European philosophy joined forces in their desire for furtherance of the idea of affirmation of life, and because they put themselves at the service of society, could the seventeenth and eighteenth centuries develop the civilization of which we are the beneficiaries.

Yet, as the negation of the world and life were rejected in the eighteenth century, certain tendencies evident in the Middle Ages and post–Middle Ages reappeared. Christianity ceased to be a creative force in civilization, as we have ample opportunity to see in our own times.

In Hinduism affirmation never overcame the negative attitude toward life and the world. In India a break with the traditional pessimism never occurred like the one brought about by powerful thinkers in the Christianity of the sixteenth, seventeenth, and eighteenth centuries. In spite of its ethical aspirations, Hinduism, therefore, was never in a position to accomplish in the Orient what Christianity was able to do for civilization in the same period.

Islam can be called a world religion only by virtue of its broad base. Spiritually it could not develop fully, because it was not based on any deep thought of the world or mankind. If ever any such thought stirred within it, it was suppressed in order to maintain the authority of tradition. Nevertheless the Islam of today carries within it stronger tendencies toward mysticism and greater ethical depth than appears on the surface.

While I was busy with these studies, a few days before Christmas, 1919, I received an invitation from Archbishop Nathan Söderblom to deliver some lectures after Easter for the Olaus-Petri Foundation at the University of Uppsala. The invitation came as a complete surprise. In my isolation at Strasbourg, ever since the war I had felt rather like a coin that has rolled under a piece of furniture and has been forgotten there. Only once—in October 1919—had I been in touch with the outer world. With great difficulty I obtained a passport and visa and, scraping together every penny I could, I went to Barcelona to let my friends from the Orfeó Catalá once more hear me play the organ. This first foray into the world allowed me to see that as an artist I was still appreciated.

On the return journey from Tarascon to Lyons, I had as fellow passengers some sailors belonging to the cruiser *Ernest Renan*. When I asked them what sort of man it was whose name they had on their caps, they answered: "We've never been told; it's probably the name of some dead general."

In academic circles I could have believed myself entirely forgotten but for the affection and kindness of the theologians at Zürich and Bern.

For my lectures in Uppsala I chose as subject the problem of affirmation of the world and of ethics in philosophy and world religions. When I began work on the lectures I was still without my chapters from *The Philosophy of Civilization* that had been left behind in Africa, so I had to write them over again. At first I was very unhappy about this, but I later realized that this repetition was not unprofitable, and I became reconciled to my fate. It was not until the summer of 1920, after my return from Uppsala, that the manuscript from Africa at last reached me.

In Uppsala for the first time I found an echo of the thoughts I had been carrying about with me for five years. In the last lecture, in which I developed the fundamental ideas of the principle of Reverence for Life, I was so moved that I found it difficult to speak.

I came to Sweden a tired, depressed, and still ailing man—for in the summer of 1919 I had had to undergo a second operation. In the magnificent air of Uppsala and the kind atmosphere of the archbishop's house, in which my wife and I were guests, I recovered my health and once more found joy in my work.

But there still weighed on me the burden of the debts I had contracted with the Paris Missionary Society and Parisian acquaintances to keep the hospital open during the war. While we were walking together, the archbishop learned of my worries and suggested I give organ recitals and lectures in Sweden, a country in which considerable wealth had accumulated during the war. He also gave me introductions in several cities.

Elias Söderström, a student of theology (who died as a missionary a few years later), offered to be my traveling companion. Standing by me on the platform or in the pulpit he translated my lectures on the forest hospital, sentence by sentence, in such a lively way that in a few moments the audience had forgotten that they were listening to a translation. How fortunate that in the services at Lambaréné I had acquired the art of speaking through an interpreter.

The essential technique involves speaking in short, simple, and clearly constructed sentences, very carefully going through the talk with the interpreter beforehand, and faithfully following the version with which he is familiar. With this preparation the interpreter has to make no effort to understand the meaning of the sentence being translated; he catches it like a ball that he relays immediately to the listeners. By following this plan it is possible to deliver even scientific papers through an interpreter. It is much better than for the speaker to inflict on himself and his hearers the torture of speaking in a language he only knows imperfectly.

Though they are not large, the wonderfully resonant old Swedish organs pleased me greatly. They were admirably adapted to my method of rendering Bach's music.

In the course of a few weeks I had earned through concerts and lectures so much money that I could pay off the most pressing of my debts.

When in the middle of July I left Sweden, where my experience had been so happy, I firmly made up my mind to resume my work at Lambaréné. Until then I had not ventured to think of it, but had instead considered the idea of returning to a university career. Some hints before my departure for Sweden pointed to Switzerland as the country where this might be possible. In 1920 I was made an Honorable Doctor of Divinity by the theological faculty at Zürich.

The Book of African Reminiscences

17

At home again I set to work at once writing down my recollections of Africa under the title *Zwischen Wasser und Urwald (On the Edge of the Primeval Forest)*. The Lindblad publishing house in Uppsala had commissioned me to write such a book, but it was not an easy task for they had restricted me to a given number of words. When I had finished I had to cut several thousand words, and that process was more difficult than writing the entire book. In the end, the complete chapter about the timber trade in the jungle would have had to have been dropped, but after my urgent pleas the publisher accepted the manuscript with this supplementary section still intact.

That I was compelled to count words for that book was good for me. Since then I have disciplined myself—even in my *Philosophy of Civilization*—to achieve the greatest possible economy of expression.

Zwischen Wasser und Urwald appeared in Swedish, translated by Baroness Greta Lagerfelt, in 1921. In the same year it came out in German (first in Switzerland), and then in English with the title *On the Edge of the Primeval Forest*, translated by my friend C. T. Campion. Later on it was published in Dutch, French, Danish, and Finnish.

It was illustrated mainly with photographs by Richard Classen of Hamburg. In 1914 he had been in Lambaréné purchasing lumber, and later I supplied him with medicines when he was a prisoner of war.

To give an account of my activity in a West African primeval forest gave me a chance to express views on the difficult problems among primitive people caused by colonization.

Have we whites the right to impose our rule on primitive and semiprimitive peoples? My answer to this question is based only on my own experience before and after World War I. No, if we want only to rule and draw material advantage from their country. Yes, if we seriously desire to educate them and help them to attain a state of well-being. If there was any possibility that these peoples could live by and for themselves, we should leave them to themselves. It is, however, a fact that world trade has penetrated these areas to such an extent that the clock cannot be turned back. Through world trade they have lost their freedom. The economic and social conditions under which the African people once lived have been destroyed. An inevitable result has been that the chiefs, using the weapons and money that commerce has placed at their disposal, have reduced most of their people to servitude and turned them into slaves who must work for the benefit of a small minority controlling the export trade.

Sometimes, as in the days of the slave trade, the people themselves have become merchandise to be exchanged for money, lead, gunpowder, tobacco, and brandy.

That many among those who took possession of colonial territories committed injustice, violence, and cruelty is only too true, and this puts a heavy burden of responsibility on us. And still today the harm we inflict on the Africans should not be passed over in silence or concealed. To grant independence to the native peoples in our colonies now would inevitably lead to exploitation by their own countrymen and would in no way make up for our failures.

Our only possible course is to exercise the power we have for the benefit of the native people and thus justify morally what we do. Even colonization can allege some acts of moral value. It has put an end to the slave trade; it has stopped the perpetual wars that the African peoples formerly waged with one another, and it has thus established a lasting peace in large portions of the world. It endeavors in many ways to produce in the colonies conditions that render more difficult the exploitation of the population by world trade. I dare not picture what the lot of the native lumbermen in the forests of the Ogowe district would be if the government authorities, who at the present time protect their rights against the merchants, both white and black, were withdrawn.

The tragic fact is that the interests of colonization and those of civilization do not necessarily run parallel, but are often in direct opposition to each other. It would be best if primitive people were to withdraw as much as possible from world commerce. Then under judicious administration they could gradually move from a nomadic or seminomadic life to a settled existence as farmers and artisans. That, however, is impossible because the people themselves refuse to walk away from the chance of earning money by selling goods on the world market, just as world trade is not likely to refrain from purchasing raw materials from them in exchange for manufactured goods. Thus it becomes very difficult to pursue a program of colonization that would lead toward a real civilization. These people could achieve true wealth if they could develop their agriculture and trade to meet their own needs. Instead they are only interested in producing what the world market requires, and for which it pays well. With the money thus obtained they procure from it manufactured goods and processed food, thereby making home industry unnecessary, and often even endangering the stability of their own agriculture. This is the condition in which all primitive and semiprimitive peoples who can offer to world trade rice, cotton, coffee, cocoa, minerals, timber, and other products find themselves.

Whenever the timber trade is good, famine reigns in the Ogowe region, because the villagers abandon their farms to fell as many trees as possible. In the swamps and the forest in which they find this work they live on imported rice and imported processed foods, which they purchase with the proceeds of their labor.

Civilized colonization must make an effort to avoid employing anyone for the export trade whose labor is needed in the domestic market, especially in agriculture. The sparser the population of a colony, the more difficult it is to reconcile the healthy development of the area with the interests of world trade. An increasing export trade does not always prove that a colony is making progress; it can as easily mean that it is on its way to ruin.

Road and railway construction also creates a difficult problem among local populations. Roads and railways are necessary to end the horrible custom of portage, to bring food to regions threatened by famine, and to develop the trade of the country. At the same time there is a danger that they may imperil the prosperity of the country. They do so when they demand more labor than the country can normally accommodate. Account must be taken, too, of the fact that colonial road and railway construction involves great loss of human life, even when—and this is unfortunately not always the case—the best possible provision is made for the lodging and board of the laborers. It can also happen that the district the road or the railway was meant to serve is instead ruined by it. The opening up of any region must therefore be embarked upon with the greatest care. Whatever the plan projected, it must be implemented gradually, perhaps even with interruptions so the project can be reviewed. Experience has shown that in this way many lives can be saved.

In the interests of developing the country it may become necessary to transplant remote villages nearer to the railway or the road. But only when no other course is possible should there be interference of this kind, or with any of the human rights of the local people.

How much disaffection is caused again and again in the colonies by regulations issued by some official who wants to draw attention to himself! With regard to the much debated issue of forced labor, I feel strongly that the Africans should under no circumstances be forced by the authorities to work, whether for a short or longer period, whether for private enterprise or as compensation for taxes. People should only be asked to perform tasks that are in the public interest, and this should be supervised by state officials. We should never force the African to work by demanding ever-increasing taxes. He will, of course, have to work in order to pay taxes, but hidden forced labor will no more change him from an idle into an industrious man than open demands. Injustice cannot produce a moral result.

In every colony in the world today the taxes are already so high that they can be paid by the population only with difficulty. Without much thought, colonies everywhere have been burdened with loans the interest on which can hardly be raised.

The problems of educating people are related to economic and social problems and are no less complicated. Farming and crafts are the foundations of civilization. Only where that foundation exists can a portion of the population engage in commercial and intellectual professions.

It is the misfortune of all colonies—and not only of those with primitive or semiprimitive populations—that those who go through the schools are then for the most part lost to agriculture and crafts. Instead of contributing to the development of both, the change of status has led to unhealthy economic and social conditions. Constructive colonization means educating the local people in such a way that they are not alienated from agriculture and crafts but attracted to them. Intellectual learning should be accompanied in every colonial school by the acquisition of every kind of manual skill. For their civilization it is important that the Africans learn to bake bricks, to build, to saw logs into planks, to be ready with hammer, plane, and chisel.

But the most important thing of all is that we stop the annihilation of the primitive and semiprimitive peoples. Their existence is threatened by alcohol, which commerce provides, by diseases we have taken to them, and by diseases that had already existed among them but which, like sleeping sickness, were first spread by the traffic that colonization brought with it. Today that disease is a peril to millions.

The harm that the importation of alcohol brings to these

people cannot be remedied by forbidding brandy and rum while allowing wine and beer as before. In the colonies wine and beer are much more dangerous beverages than in Europe, because, to preserve them in tropical and subtropical regions, pure alcohol is always added. The absence of brandy and rum is amply made up for by an enormously increased consumption of this fortified wine and beer. The only way to prevent the damage that alcohol brings to these people is to completely prohibit all alcoholic beverages.

In nearly all colonies the struggle against disease has been undertaken with too little energy and was begun too late. The need to bring medical help to the people in our colonies is frequently argued on the ground that it is worthwhile to preserve the "human resource" without which the colonies would lose their value. In reality, however, the issue is quite different. It is unthinkable that we civilized peoples should keep for ourselves alone those means for fighting sickness, pain, and death that science has given us. If there is any ethical thinking at all among us, how can we refuse to let these new discoveries benefit those in distant lands who are subject to even greater physical distress than we are? In addition to the physicians who are sent out by the governments, and of whom there are never enough to accomplish a fraction of what needs doing, other doctors must go out to the colonies as a humane duty mandated by the conscience of society. Whoever among us has learned through personal experience what pain and anxiety really are must help to ensure that those out there who are in physical need obtain the same help that once came to him. He no longer belongs to himself alone; he has become the brother of all who suffer. It is this "brotherhood of those who bear the mark of pain" that demands humane medical services for the colonies. Commissioned by their representatives, medical people must do for the suffering in far-off lands what cries out to be done in the name of true civilization.

It was because I relied on the elementary truth embodied in this idea, the "brotherhood of those who bear the mark of pain," that I ventured to found the forest hospital at Lambaréné.

Finally, I must insist that whatever benefit we confer upon the peoples of our colonies is not charity, but atonement for the terrible sufferings we white people have inflicted upon them ever since the day our first ship found its way to their shores. The colonial problems that exist today cannot be solved by political measures alone. A new element must be introduced; white and black must meet in an atmosphere infused with an ethical spirit. Only then will communication be possible.

Günsbach and
Journeys Abroad

18

On the Sunday before Palm Sunday in 1921, I had the pleasure of playing the organ at the premiere of Bach's *St. Matthew Passion* at the Orfeó Catalá in Barcelona—the very first time this work was performed in Spain.

In April 1921, I resigned my two posts at Strasbourg, hoping that I could live in the future by my pen and my organ recitals. In order to work in peace on *The Philosophy of Civilization* I moved with my wife and child—a daughter born to us on January 14, my own birthday, in 1919— to my father's vicarage at Günsbach.

197

For a pied-à-terre in Strasbourg, where I often had to spend considerable periods of time using the library, I had an attic room at the home of Pastor Dietz-Härter's widow, who lived in an old house in the rue d'ail (Garlic Street).

My work was often interrupted by travel. Various universities invited me to give lectures on the philosophy of civilization or on the problems of primitive Christianity. Through lectures about the hospital at Lambaréné I raised funds for its continuation. With organ recitals I was able to secure my own and my family's future after I returned to Africa.

In the autumn of 1921 I was in Switzerland, and from there I went in November to Sweden. At the end of January I left Sweden for Oxford to deliver the Dale Memorial Lectures at Mansfield College. After that I lectured at Selly Oak College in Birmingham (on "Christianity and the Religions of the World"), at Cambridge (on "The Significance of Eschatology"), and in London to the Society for the Study of Religion (on "The Pauline Problem"). I also gave a number of organ recitals in England.

In the middle of March 1922, I returned to Sweden from England to give more concerts and lectures. No sooner was I home than I set forth again for weeks to give lectures and concerts in Switzerland.

In the summer of 1922 I was allowed to work on *The Philosophy of Civilization* undisturbed. In the autumn I went again to Switzerland, and after that I gave some lectures on ethics at Copenhagen at the invitation of the university's department of theology. These were followed by organ recitals and lectures in various towns of Denmark.

In January 1923, I lectured on the philosophy of civilization at Prague, at the invitation of Professor Oscar Kraus. I thus began a warm friendship with that loyal pupil of Brentano.

How wonderful were the experiences of these years! When I first went to Africa I prepared to make three sacrifices: to abandon the organ; to renounce academic teaching activities, to which I had become quite attached; and to lose my financial independence and rely for the rest of my life on the help of friends.

I had begun to make these three sacrifices, and only my intimate friends knew what they cost me. But then it happened to me what happened to Abraham when he prepared to sacrifice his son. Like him, I was spared the sacrifice. Thanks to my good health and thanks to the piano with the attached pedals that the Bach Society of Paris had given me as a present, I had been able to maintain my organ technique in the tropical climate. During the many peaceful hours I was able to spend with Bach during my four and a half years in the jungle I had penetrated deeper into the spirit of his works. I returned to Europe, therefore, not as an artist who had become an amateur, but in full possession of my technique.

For the renunciation of my teaching activities at the University of Strasbourg I found compensation in opportunities for lecturing at many other universities. So if I did for a time lose my financial independence, I was now able to win it back again with the organ and my books. The fact that I was spared the triple sacrifice that I had already made sustained me through all the difficulties the postwar years brought to me and to so many others. I was prepared to face hard work and renunciation.

In the spring of 1923 the first two volumes of *The Philosophy of Civilization* were completed, and they were published that same year. The first bears the title *Verfall und Wiederaufbau der Kultur* (*The Decay and Restoration of Civilization*) and the second *Kultur und Ethik* (*Civilization and Ethics*).

The terms *moral* and *ethical* are basically synonymous. They define whatever conforms to established custom. *Moral* derives from the Latin and *ethic* from the Greek. In general use the term *morals* relates to moral precepts and conduct, while *ethics* comprises the science of morals and scholarship on notions of the Good.

In the book on *The Decay and Restoration of Civilization* I describe the relationship between civilization and worldview.

I show that the philosophy of the nineteenth century is responsible for the decline of civilization. It did not know how to keep alive the concern for civilization that existed in the period of the Enlightenment. It should have continued the unfinished work of the eighteenth century and explained the natural, fundamental bond between ethics and our concept of the world. Instead the nineteenth century lost itself in the nonessential. It abandoned man's natural quest for a concept of the world, and instead developed the science of the history of philosophy. It developed a worldview based on history and the natural sciences. This view was, however, without vigor and incapable of sustaining a strong civilization.

Just at the time when the philosophy of civilization lost its power, it was threatened by another danger. The machine age created living conditions that made it difficult for civilization to progress. And because men had no ethical concept of the world, civilization declined.

Overburdened with work, modern man has lost his ability to concentrate, has lost his spirituality in all spheres. The false interpretation of events in history and real life leads to a nationalism in which humanitarian ideals have no place. Our thoughts must, therefore, be directed toward a concept of the world that is inspired by the ideals of true civilization. If we begin to reflect at all on ethics and our spiritual relationship to the universe, we are already on the road leading back from the uncivilized to civilization.

Civilization I define in quite general terms as spiritual and material progress in all spheres of life, accompanied by the ethical development of individuals and of mankind.

In my book *Civilization and Ethics,* I describe the tragic struggle of European thought to attain an ethical concept of the world and life. I would have liked to include the struggle toward a philosophy of civilization as it has developed in the world religions. But I had to abandon this plan because it would have made the book too long. I therefore limited myself to a few brief allusions to the subject.

I intentionally avoided technical philosophical terminology. I wanted to appeal to thinking men and women and to provoke them into basic thought about the questions of existence that are in the minds of every human being.

What is it that takes place in the vain struggle toward a deep ethical affirmation of life and the world? Socrates made a great effort to represent the ethical as the reasonable and to understand the world and life affirmation as having some meaning. But by an inexorable logic this led to resignation. The ideal of Stoic philosophy is the wise man who retires from this world.

It is only in the later Stoicism of Marcus Aurelius, Epictetus, Seneca, and others that a confident ethical concept develops that imposes on the individual the duty to work in the world to create better material and spiritual conditions and to cultivate humanitarian ideals.

This late Stoic view of the world is to a certain extent the forerunner of what in the eighteenth century was accepted as "conforming to reason." When it first appears on the stage of history it does not yet have the strength to establish its position or to release its reforming powers. It is true the great Stoic rulers are devoted to it, and under its influence they attempt to arrest the decadence of the ancient world, which began in late antiquity. Their vision, however, never gained any influence over the masses.

How do the late Stoicism and the rationalism of the eighteenth century lead to an ethical affirmation of the world? Not by accepting the world as it is, but by conceiving the course of world events as the expression of a rational, ethical world will. The world-accepting ethical will of man interprets the forces that are active in the course of history according to his own common sense. Instead of offering an objective concept of the world, this attitude projects ethical impulses.

This process is repeated wherever philosophy comes to an ethical acceptance of the world. It deduces this principle from an interpretation of the course of world history that seeks to make this course intelligible, as having meaning and being in some way or other directed to ethical ends. Humans, through their own ethical actions, can now serve the overall purpose of the universe.

In Cong-tse and Zarathustra the ethical affirmation of life is supported by a worldview founded on the same hypothesis.

Kant, Fichte, Hegel, and the other great thinkers of speculative philosophy were not satisfied with the simple and naive theories of moral rationalism of the eighteenth century. They arrived at their conclusions through more complicated operations of thought. They stated that the ethical affirmative view of life can only be reached through a correct theory of knowledge, or the logical comprehension of the original "Being" within the context of world events in space and time.

In the artificial complexity of the great systems, the educated minds of the early nineteenth century assumed that they had proof that the ethic of life affirmation was the logical result of rational thought. Their joy, however, was of short duration. Around the middle of the century these logical castles in the air crumbled and collapsed under the pressure of a realistic and scientific method of thinking. A period of severe disenchantment set in. Reason gave up all its attempts to make this world comprehensible either by manipulation or by force. It was ready to resign itself and come to terms with reality as it is, drawing from it motives for action that are consonant with an ethical acceptance of the world. But it soon learned from experience that reality refuses to provide what is expected of it. Reason alone cannot provide an interpretation of the world that assigns a course of ethical action for man.

Reason could not immediately understand its limitations. It was, however, evident that from that moment on the old ethical ideals had lost their vitality. Any attempt that reason might have made to restore the old positions through rational interpretation of the world were doomed to fail.

The philosophy of Reverence for Life takes the world as it is. And the world means the horrible in the glorious, the meaningless in the fullness of meaning, the sorrowful in the joyful. Whatever our own point of view the world will remain for us an enigma.

But that does not mean that we need stand before the problem of life at our wits' end, because we have to renounce all hope of seeing the course of world events as having any meaning. Reverence for Life leads us into a spiritual relationship with the world independent of a full understanding of the universe. Through the dark valley of resignation it takes us by an inward necessity up to the shining heights of ethical acceptance of the world.

We are no longer obliged to derive our ethical worldview from knowledge of the universe. In the principle of Reverence for Life we possess a concept of the world founded on itself. It renews itself in us every time we reflect thoughtfully about ourselves and our relation to life around us. It is not through knowledge, but through experience of the world that we are brought into relationship with it.

All thinking that penetrates to the bottom arrives at ethical mysticism. What is rational reaches eventually the nonrational. The ethical mysticism of Reverence for Life is rational thought that derives its power from the spiritual nature of our being.

While I was still correcting the proofs of *Civilization and Ethics*, I had already begun packing the cases for my second voyage to Africa.

In the autumn of 1923 the printing was interrupted for a time because the print shop belonging to the publisher of the German edition, which was located in Nördlingen (Bavaria), was requisitioned by the state to help in the production of the paper money needed during the inflation.

That I was able to take up my work in the jungle again I owed to friends in Alsace, Switzerland, Sweden, Denmark, England, and Czechoslovakia, who had decided to help me financially after they had heard my lectures.

Before leaving for Africa I also prepared for publication the lectures I had delivered at Selly Oak College in Birmingham on "Christianity and the Religions of the World." In the lectures I try to define the nature of religions from the philosophic standpoint and to analyze the role that the affirmation as well as the negation of life and ethics play in them.

Unfortunately I did not have enough time to synthesize my research on world religions, and I therefore had to publish the lectures just as I had delivered them.

In the haste of packing, I also quietly wrote my childhood recollections owing to a visit to my friend Dr. O. Pfister, the well-known Zürich psychoanalyst. Early in the summer of 1923, while traveling across Switzerland from west to east, I had a two-hour wait in Zürich and went to visit him. He offered me refreshment and gave me an opportunity to stretch out and rest. Then he asked me to narrate some incidents of my childhood just as they came into my mind. He wanted to use them for a young people's magazine. Soon afterward he sent me a copy of what he had taken down in shorthand during those two hours. I asked him not to publish it, but to leave it to me to complete. Then, one Sunday afternoon shortly before my departure for Africa, when it was alternately raining and snowing, I wrote, as an epilogue to what I had told him, some thoughts about what used to stir me when I looked back upon my youth. This manuscript was published under the title *Aus meiner Kindheit und Jugendzeit (Memoirs of Childhood and Youth).*

The Second Period in Africa, 1924–1927

19

On February 14, 1924, I left Strasbourg. My wife could not go with me this time because of her poor health. I have never ceased to be grateful to her that, under these circumstances, she made the sacrifice of consenting to my resuming work at Lambaréné. I was accompanied by Noel Gillespie, a young Oxford student of chemistry. His mother had entrusted him to me for a few months as a helper.

When we embarked at Bordeaux I came under the suspicions of the customs officer who was inspecting travelers' baggage. I had with me four potato sacks full of unanswered letters, which I meant to answer during the voyage. He had never encountered a traveler with so many letters, and because at that time the transfer of French money to other countries was strictly forbidden—a traveler was only allowed to take five thousand francs with him—he could not help but suspect that money was hidden among those letters. He therefore spent an hour and a half examining them, one by one, until, at the bottom of the second sack, he gave up, shaking his head.

After a long voyage on the Dutch cargo boat *Orestes*, which gave me an opportunity to get to know the places along the west coast, we arrived at Lambaréné at dawn on Saturday, April 19, the day before Easter.

All that still remained of the hospital were the small building of corrugated iron and the hardwood skeleton of one of the big bamboo huts. During the seven years of my absence all the other buildings had decayed and collapsed. The path leading from the hospital to the doctor's bungalow on the hill was so completely overgrown with grass and creepers that I could scarcely trace its windings.

The first job, then, was to make the minimal necessary repairs on the rotten and leaky roofs of the bungalow and the two hospital buildings that were still standing. Next I reerected the fallen buildings, a job that took me several months. This work was so exhausting that I was quite unable to give my evenings to working over the manuscript of *The Mysticism of Paul the Apostle*, begun in 1911, as I had planned. I had brought it for the second time to Africa.

My life during those months was lived as a doctor in

For protecting the hospital against river floods and from the torrents that washed down from the hills after heavy storms, I became a modern prehistoric man and erected it as a village of corrugated iron on piles.

The professional work in the hospital I left almost entirely to my colleagues, Dr. Nessmann (an Alsatian), Dr. Lauterburg (a Swiss), and Dr. Trensz (an Alsatian who came to relieve Dr. Nessmann). I myself for a year and a half became overseer of the laborers who cut down the trees on the chosen site and worked on the buildings.

I had to assume this function because of the ever-changing squad of "volunteers" recruited from among the companions of the patients as well as convalescents well enough to work. They would acknowledge no authority save that of the "old" Doctor. While I was foreman of a troop of workmen hewing down trees, the news reached me that the philosophy faculty of the University of Prague had conferred on me an honorary doctoral degree.

As soon as the building site had been cleared, I started preparing the land near it for cultivation. What a joy it was to win fields from the jungle!

Year after year since then, work has been carried on with the object of producing a Garden of Eden around the hospital. Hundreds of young fruit trees, which we have grown from seed, have already been planted. Someday there will be so much fruit growing here that all can take what they want, and there will be no need to steal. We have already reached this stage with the papaya, the mango, and the oil palms. The papayas now produce more fruit than the hospital needs. There were so many mangoes and oil palms in the woods already that, once we cut down the other trees, they formed regular groves. As soon as they were freed from the creepers that were strangling them and from the giant trees that overshadowed them, they at once began to bear fruit.

These fruit trees were, of course, not part of the virgin forest. The mangoes had made their way into the forest from the villages that once stood along the riverbank; the oil palms had sprung up from kernels that the parrots had carried off from the trees near the villages and then had dropped. The jungle of equatorial Africa contains no indigenous trees with edible fruits. The traveler whose supplies give out during his journey is doomed to starvation. It is well known that the clumps of banana and manioc, the oil palms, the mango trees, and much of the other vegetation that supplies edible food are not indigenous to equatorial Africa, but were introduced by Europeans from the West Indian islands and other tropical countries.

Unfortunately fruit cannot be stored here on account of the dampness and the heat. As soon as it is picked it begins to rot. For the large number of plantains required for feeding the patients I still have to resort to supplies from the neighboring villages. The bananas, which I grow with paid labor, cost me in fact much more than those the Africans sell me from their own plantations located conveniently near the river. The Africans, however, have scarcely any fruit trees because they do not live permanently in one place, but constantly move their villages to some new site.

Since even bananas cannot be stored, I have also had to keep a considerable stock of rice on hand in case there are not enough bearing banana trees in the neighborhood.

The fact that I did not at once begin building a new hospital, but instead rebuilt the old one, was by no means a misfortune. It enabled us to accumulate experience that was now very useful. We had only one native worker who stayed with us all through the rebuilding, a carpenter named Monenzali. Without him I could not have carried out the undertaking. During the last few months I had also the help of a young carpenter from Switzerland.

My plan to return to Europe at the end of two years could not be realized. I had to stay in Africa for three and a half. In the evenings I found myself so exhausted from the continual running around in the sun that I could not write. My remaining energy lasted for nothing beyond regular practice on my piano with its pedal attachment. *The Mysticism of Paul the Apostle* therefore remained unfinished.

This second period of activity in Africa is described in the newsletter *Mitteilungen aus Lambaréné*. They contain sketches written at intervals for the information of friends of the hospital.

During my absence the work that had to be done to support the hospital was in the hands of Reverend Hans Bauer, D.D., at Basel, and my brother-in-law, Reverend Albert Woytt at Oberhausbergen, near Strasbourg.

Since 1919 Mme Emmy Martin at Strasbourg had also been closely associated with our work. In 1929 she centralized everything concerning Lambaréné and my other activities in the new house at Günsbach. Without her untiring help and that of other friends, the undertaking, now so much expanded, could not have continued.

Some of the new buildings were finished, and on January 21, 1927, the patients could be transferred from the old to the new hospital. On the evening of the last journey we made, I took the mental patients with me. Their guardians never tired of telling them that in the new hospital they would live in cells with wood floors. In the old cells the floor had been just the damp earth.

When I made my tour of the hospital that evening, there resounded from every fire and every mosquito net the greeting "It's a good hut, Doctor, a very good hut!" So now for the first time since I began to work in Africa my patients were housed as human beings should be.

In April 1927, I was able to hand over the supervision of the workers engaged in the clearing of the woods around the hospital to Mrs. C. E. B. Russell. She had just arrived from England, and she had a talent for getting the men to follow her orders. Under her leadership a beginning was also made in laying out a plantation. Since then I have noticed that on the whole the authority of a white woman is more readily recognized by the Africans than that of us men.

Around the middle of the summer in the same year I completed several additional wards. Now I was in possession of a hospital in which, if need be, we could accommodate 200 patients and those who accompanied them. In recent months the number has been between 140 and 160. Provision was also made for the isolation of dysentery patients. The building for the mental patients was erected from a fund established by the Guildhouse congregation in London in memory of a deceased member, Mr. Ambrose Pomeroy-Cragg.

Finally, after the essential interior installations were completed, I could depart for Europe and leave the responsibility for the hospital to my colleagues. On July 21 I left Lambaréné. Miss Mathilde Kottmann, who had worked at the hospital since 1924, and the sister of Dr. Lauterburg traveled with me. Miss Emma Hausknecht remained at Lambaréné, and several other nurses soon joined her to assist her in her work.

The hospital could never have existed without the assistance of the volunteers who have given of themselves so generously.

Two Years in Europe. *The Mysticism of Paul the Apostle*

20

Of the two years I spent in Europe a good part was taken up with traveling to give lectures and organ recitals. The autumn and winter of 1927 I spent in Sweden and Denmark. In the spring and early summer of 1928 I was in Holland and England; in the autumn and winter in Switzerland, Germany, and Czechoslovakia. In 1929 I undertook several recital tours in Germany. When not traveling, I lived with my wife and daughter at the mountain health resort of Königsfeld in the Black Forest, or at Strasbourg.

I had many worries due to the relatively frequent need to replace doctors and nurses in Lambaréné. Some could not tolerate the climate; others had family obligations that forced them to return to Europe sooner than they had intended. I recruited several new people, Dr. Mündler, Dr. Hediger, Dr. Stalder, and Dr. Schnabel, all from Switzerland. We were all much saddened by the death of a Swiss doctor, Dr. Eric Dölken who, in October 1929 on the voyage to Lambaréné, died suddenly in the harbor of Grand Bassam, probably from a heart attack.

I dedicated all my spare time in Europe to the completion of my book on *The Mysticism of Paul the Apostle*. I did not wish to take the manuscript with me to Africa a third time, and I soon found myself once more at home with the subject matter. Slowly the manuscript developed, chapter by chapter.

Paul's mysticism of being-in-Christ finds its explanation in the conception the Apostle has of the coming of the Messianic Kingdom and of the end of the world. On the strength of the views that he, like his fellow believers in those earliest days, had taken over from Judaism, he supposes that those who believe in Jesus as the coming Messiah will live with Him in the Messianic Kingdom in a supernatural existence, while their unbelieving contemporaries and the people of previous generations ever since the Creation must remain for some time in the grave. It is only at the close of the Messianic Kingdom, which, though supernatural, is nevertheless conceived as transitory, that, in accordance with the late Jewish view, the General Resurrection takes place and is followed by the Last Judgment. Not until then does Eternity begin, in which God "is all in all," that is, all things return to God.

Paul explains that those who see in Jesus the Messiah and who ascend to the Messianic Kingdom—in this way experiencing the resurrection before other human beings— are thus privileged because they have lived in fellowship with Jesus. Their faith in Him makes plain that God has chosen them to be the companions of the Messiah. By virtue of this union with Jesus, which is both mystical and natural, the forces that led Him to choose His death and His resurrection begin to work in them.

These believers cease to be natural men like others. They become beings who are in the process of changing from a natural to a supernatural condition. Their human appearance is only a kind of veil, which they will throw off when the Messianic Kingdom comes to pass. In a mysterious way they are already dead and have risen with Christ and in Him, and will soon share with Him the existence that follows His resurrection.

The mysticism involved in "being-in-Christ" and of having "died and risen with Christ" is extended in the eschatological expectation. The belief in the imminent manifestation of the Kingdom leads, in Paul's thought, to a conviction that, with the death and resurrection of Jesus, the change of the natural into the supernatural has already begun. We therefore deal with a mysticism that is based on the assumption of a great cosmic event.

Because Paul understood the significance of this union with Christ, he wanted to put the ethic of this union into practice. In Judaism believers had only to obey the Law, since that is valid for natural men. For the same reason it must not be imposed on heathen who have come to believe in Christ. Whoever enters into union with Christ discerns what is ethical directly from the spirit of Christ in which he shares.

For other believers inspired words and ecstasy are the surest proof of the living spirit, but Paul turns the doctrine of the spirit to ethics. According to him the spirit that believers possess is the spirit of Jesus, in which they have become participants because of the mysterious fellowship with Him that they enjoy. This spirit of Jesus is the divine force of life that prepares them for existence after the resurrection. At the same time it is the power compelling believers, because they are different, to accept themselves as men who have ceased to belong to this world. The highest manifestation of the spirit is love. Love is eternal, and men can possess it here on earth.

Thus in the eschatological mysticism of the fellowship with Christ, everything metaphysical has an ethical significance. Paul establishes the supremacy of the ethical in religion for all time in the saying "And now abideth faith, hope, and love, these three, but the greatest of these is love." He demonstrates this ethical view of what it is to be a Christian by his complete dedication to service.

Paul interprets the saying of Jesus about bread and wine being His body and blood as being in accordance with his doctrine of the mystical fellowship with Christ. He explains the significance of the Last Supper by saying that those who eat and drink enter into communion with Jesus. Baptism, the beginning of redemption through Christ, is for him the beginning of dying and rising again with Christ. The doctrine of justification by faith, which has been accepted for centuries as the essential element of Paul's thought, is in reality a concept from the primitive doctrine of the atoning death of Jesus, inspired by the mystical communion with Jesus.

In order to meet his Jewish-Christian opponents more successfully, Paul undertakes to formulate the belief in the atoning significance of the sacrifice of Jesus in such a way that this belief makes certain that the Law is no longer valid. He also rejects—in contrast to the Jewish Christians—the significance of good works, emphasized by Jewish Law, because in his mysticism he demands ethical deeds as proof of fellowship with Christ.

The doctrine of justification by faith created in order to combat Jewish Christianity has acquired great importance. Since that time those who rebelled against the concept of a Christianity justified by good works could appeal to the doctrine of the Apostle and win their case on his authority.

On the other hand the artificial logic Paul uses in his attempt to represent this doctrine as contained in the Old Testament has given rise to an erroneous criticism of him. He is accused of being the man who invented a complicated dogma to replace the simple Gospel of Jesus. In reality, however, Paul, in spite of rabbinic elements that show up here and there in his argument, is a powerful thinker who arrives at elemental truths.

He puts forward the simple Gospel of Jesus, not in the letter, but in the spirit. By raising the eschatological belief in Jesus and the Kingdom of God to the mysticism of fellowship with Christ, Paul has endowed it with a force that enables it to outlast the decline of the eschatological expectation and to be recognized by and integrated into various systems of thought as an ethical Christ-mysticism. In fact, he develops his eschatological faith to its last consequences, and he arrives at thoughts about our relation to Jesus that, because of their spiritual and ethical significance are definite and timeless, in spite of the fact that they originated from the metaphysics of eschatology.

There is, then, no Greek element in Paul. He does, however, give the Christian faith a form that can be assimilated by the Greek spirit. Ignatius and Justin, in whose thought this process is completed, translate the mysticism of fellowship with Christ into Greek concepts.

I wrote the last chapter of *The Mysticism of Paul the Apostle* in December 1929, on board ship between Bordeaux and Cape Lopez. The introduction was written the day after Christmas on board the river steamer that took us—my wife and myself, Dr. Anna Schmitz, and Miss Marie Secretan, who came to work in the laboratory—to Lambaréné.

On this third arrival I unfortunately again found that construction work had to be done. During a serious epidemic of dysentery, which was coming to an end just as I arrived, the wards of the unit had proved to be too small. As a result, the neighboring building for mental patients had to be turned over to those suffering from dysentery, and a new one had to be erected for the mental patients. Based on the experiences accumulated in the meantime, the new buildings were made stronger and at the same time lighter and more airy than the old ones.

After that I had to build a large barrack with separate beds for severe cases, an airy and theft-proof storeroom for food supplies, and rooms for the African hospital orderlies.

With the help of Monenzali, our loyal carpenter, all this work was done in a year, while I carried on my duties in the hospital. At the same time a young Alsatian forester who spent his vacation in the Ogowe offered his competent help. He built a large cement reservoir for rainwater and an airy building of the same material, which serves us as dining room and common room.

Toward Easter, 1930, my wife, exhausted by the climate, unfortunately had to return to Europe. In the course of the summer a new Alsatian physician, Dr. Meyländer, arrived.

The hospital is now known over an area of hundreds of kilometers. People come to us for operations who must spend weeks on the journey.

Through the generosity of friends in Europe we were able to build an operating room that is outfitted with everything necessary. We now can store in the pharmacy all the medications we require, even the expensive ones needed for the treatment of tropical diseases. Further, it makes it possible for us to feed the many sick people who are too poor to buy their own food.

To work at Lambaréné is now a pleasure, the more so because we have enough doctors and nurses to do all that is needed without our having to work ourselves to the point of exhaustion. How can we thank the friends of the hospital who have made such work possible!

While work at the hospital is still demanding, it is not, as it once was, beyond our strength. In the evening I am fresh enough to turn to intellectual labor, although this leisure-time work is often still interrupted for days or even weeks at a time when I become preoccupied with surgical and serious medical cases and can think about nothing else. For this reason this simple narrative of my life and work, which I had planned as my first literary work during this present stay in Africa, is taking me many months to complete.

Epilogue

Two observations have cast their shadows over my life. One is the realization that the world is inexplicably mysterious and full of suffering, the other that I have been born in a period of spiritual decline for mankind.

I myself found the basis and the direction for my life at the moment I discovered the principle of Reverence for Life, which contains life's ethical affirmation. I therefore want to work in this world to help people to think more deeply and more independently. I am in complete disagreement with the spirit of our age, because it is filled with contempt for thought. We have come to doubt whether thinking will ever be capable of answering questions about the universe and our relationship to it in a way that would give meaning and substance to our lives.

Today, in addition to that neglect of thought, there is also a mistrust of it. The organized political, social, and religious associations of our time are at work convincing the individual not to develop his convictions through his own thinking but to assimilate the ideas they present to him. Any man who thinks for himself is to them inconvenient and even ominous. He does not offer sufficient guarantee that he will merge into the organization.

Corporate bodies do not look for their strength in ideas and in the values of the people for whom they are responsible. They try to achieve the greatest possible uniformity. They believe that in this way they hold the greatest power, offensive as well as defensive.

Hence the spirit of the age, instead of deploring the fact that thought seems to be unequal to its task, rejoices in it and gives it no credit for what, in spite of its imperfections, it has already accomplished. Against all the evidence it refuses to admit that human progress up until today has come about through the efforts of thought. It will not recognize that thought may in the future accomplish what it has not yet achieved. The spirit of the age ignores such considerations. Its only concern is to discredit individual thought in every possible way.

Man today is exposed throughout his life to influences that try to rob him of all confidence in his own thinking. He lives in an atmosphere of intellectual dependence, which surrounds him and manifests itself in everything he hears or reads. It is in the people whom he meets every day; it is in the political parties and associations that have claimed him as their own; it pervades all the circumstances of his life.

From every side and in the most varied ways it is hammered into him that the truths and convictions that he needs for life must be taken away from the associations that have rights over him. The spirit of the age never lets him find himself. Over and over again, convictions are forced upon him just as he is exposed, in big cities, to glaring neon signs of companies that are rich enough to install them and enjoin him at every step to give preference to one or another shoe polish or soup mix.

By the spirit of the age, then, the man of today is forced into skepticism about his own thinking, so that he may become receptive to what he receives from authority. He cannot resist this influence because he is overworked, distracted, and incapable of concentrating. Moreover, the material dependence that is his lot has an effect on his mind, so he finally believes that he is not qualified to come to his own conclusions.

His self-confidence is also affected by the prodigious developments in knowledge. He cannot comprehend or assimilate the new discoveries. He is forced to accept them as givens, although he does not understand them. As a result of this attitude toward scientific truth he begins to doubt his own judgment in other spheres of thought.

Thus the circumstances of the age do their best to deliver us to the spirit of the age. The seed of skepticism has germinated. In fact, modern man no longer has any confidence in himself. Behind a self-assured exterior he conceals an inner lack of confidence. In spite of his great technological achievements and material possessions, he is an altogether stunted being, because he makes no use of his capacity for thinking. It will always remain incomprehensible that our generation, which has shown itself so great by its discoveries and inventions, could fall so low in the realm of thought.

In a period that ridicules as antiquated and without value whatever seems akin to rational or independent thought, and which even mocks the inalienable human rights proclaimed in the eighteenth century, I declare myself to be one who places all his confidence in rational thinking. I venture to tell our generation that it is not at the end of rationalism just because past rationalism first gave way to romanticism and later to a pretended realism that reigned in intellectual as well as in material life. When we have passed through all the follies of the so-called universal realpolitik, and because of it suffered spiritual misery, there will be no other choice but to turn to a new rationalism more profound and more effective than that of the past. To renounce thinking is to declare mental bankruptcy.

When we give up the conviction that we can arrive at the truth through thinking, skepticism appears. Those who work toward greater skepticism in our age expect that by denouncing all hope of self-discovered truth, men will come to accept as true whatever is forced upon them by authority and by propaganda.

But their calculations are mistaken. Whoever opens the sluices to let a flood of skepticism pour over the land cannot assume that later he can stem the flood. Only a few of those who give up the search for truth will be so docile as to submit once and for all to official doctrine. The mass of people will remain skeptical. They lose all desire for truth, finding themselves quite comfortable in a life without thought, driven now here, now there, from one opinion to another.

But merely accepting authoritarian truth, even if that truth has some virtue, does not bring skepticism to an end. To blindly accept a truth one has never reflected upon retards the advance of reason. Our world rots in deceit. Our very attempt to manipulate truth itself brings us to the brink of disaster.

Truth based on a skepticism that has become belief has not the spiritual qualities of truth that originated in thought. It is superficial and inflexible. It exerts an influence over man, but it cannot reach his inner being. Living truth is only that which has its origin in thought.

Just as a tree bears the same fruit year after year and at the same time fruit that is new each year, so must all permanently valuable ideas be continually created anew in thought. But our age pretends to make a sterile tree bear fruit by tying fruits of truth onto its branches.

Only when we gain the confidence that we can find the truth through our own individual thought will we be able to arrive at living truth. Independent thought, provided it is profound, never degenerates into subjectivity. What is true in our tradition will be brought to light through deep thought, and it can become the force of reason in us. The will to sincerity must be as strong as the will to truth. Only an age that has the courage of conviction can possess truth that works as a force of spirit and of reason.

Sincerity is the foundation of the life of mind and spirit. With its disdain for thinking, our generation has lost its feeling for sincerity. It can therefore be helped only by reviving the voice of thought.

Because I have this certainty, I oppose the spirit of the age and accept with confidence the responsibility for contributing to the rekindling of the fire of thought.

The concept of Reverence for Life is by its very nature especially well qualified to take up the struggle against skepticism. It is elemental.

Elemental thinking starts from fundamental questions about the relationship of man to the universe, about the meaning of life, and about the nature of what is good. It is directly linked to the thought that motivates all people. It penetrates our thought, enlarges and deepens it, and makes it more profound.

We find such elemental thinking in Stoicism. When as a student I began to study the history of philosophy, I found it difficult to tear myself away from Stoicism and to make my way through the utterly different thinking that succeeded it. It is true that the results of Stoic thought did not satisfy me, but I had the feeling that this simple kind of philosophizing was the right one. I could not understand how people had come to abandon it.

Stoicism seemed to me great in that it goes straight for its goal, is universally intelligible and at the same time profound. It makes the best of what it recognizes as truth, even if it is not completely satisfying. It puts life into that truth by seriously devoting itself to it. It possesses the spirit of sincerity and urges men to gather their thoughts and to become more inward. It arouses in them a sense of responsibility. It also seemed to me that the fundamental tenet of Stoicism is correct, namely that man must bring himself into a spiritual relation with the world and become one with it. In its essence, Stoicism is a natural philosophy that ends in mysticism.

Just as I felt Stoicism to be elemental, so I felt that the thought of Lao-tse was the same when I became acquainted with his *Tao-te-king*. For him, too, it is important that man come, by simple thought, into a spiritual relation with the world and prove his unity with it by his life.

There is, therefore, an essential relationship between Greek Stoicism and Chinese philosophy. The difference between them is that the first had its origin in well-developed, logical thinking, the second in intuitive thinking that was undeveloped yet marvelously profound.

This elemental thinking, however, which emerges in European as in Far Eastern philosophy, has not been able to maintain the position of leadership that it should occupy within systems of thought. It is unsuccessful because its conclusions do not satisfy our needs.

Stoic thought neglects the impulse that leads to ethical acts that manifest themselves in the will to live as it evolved with the intellectual and spiritual development of man. Hence Greek Stoicism goes no further than the ideal of resignation, Lao-tse no further than the benign passivity that to us Europeans seems so curious and paradoxical.

The history of philosophy documents that the thoughts of ethical affirmation of life, which are natural to man, cannot be content with the results of simple logical thinking about man and his relationship to the universe. They cannot integrate themselves. Logical thought is forced to take detours via which it hopes to arrive at its goal. The detours logic has to take lead primarily to an interpretation of the universe in which ethical action has meaning and purpose.

In the late Stoicism of Epictetus, of Marcus Aurelius, and of Seneca, in the rationalism of the eighteenth century, and in that of Cong-tse (Confucius), Meng-tse (Mencius), Mi-tse (Micius), and other Chinese thinkers, philosophy starts from the fundamental problem of the relationship of man to the universe and reaches an ethical affirmation of life and of the world. This philosophy traces the course of world events back to a world will with ethical aims, and claims man for service to it.

In the thinking of Brahmanism and of the Buddha, in the Indian systems generally, and in the philosophy of Schopenhauer, the opposite explanation of the world is put forward, namely that the life that runs its course in space and time is purposeless and must be brought to an end. The sensible attitude of man to the world is therefore to renounce the world and life.

Side by side with the kind of thought that is concerned with elemental issues, another kind has emerged, especially in European philosophy. I call it "secondary" because it does not focus on the relationship between man and the universe. It is concerned with the problem of the nature of knowledge, with logical speculation, with natural science, with psychology, with sociology, and with other things, as if philosophy were really concerned with the answers to all these questions for their own sake, or as if it consisted merely in sifting and systematizing the results of the various sciences. Instead of urging man toward constant meditation about himself and his relationship to the world, this philosophy presents him with the results of epistemology, of logical deduction, of natural science, of psychology, or of sociology, as if it could, with the help of these disciplines, arrive at a concept of his relation with the universe.

On all these issues this "secondary" philosophy discourses with him as if he were, not a being who is in the world and lives his life in it, but one who is stationed near it and contemplates it from the outside.

Because it approaches the problem of the relationship of man to the universe from some arbitrarily chosen standpoint, or perhaps bypasses it altogether, this nonelemental European philosophy lacks unity and cohesion. It appears more or less restless, artificial, eccentric, and fragmentary. At the same time, it is the richest and most universal. In its systems, half-systems, and nonsystems, which succeed and interpenetrate each other, it is able to contemplate the problem of a philosophy of civilization from every side and every possible perspective. It is also the most practical in that it deals with the natural sciences, history, and ethical questions more profoundly than the others do.

The world philosophy of the future will not result in efforts to reconcile European and non-European thought but rather in the confrontation between elemental and nonelemental thinking.

Mysticism is not part of intellectual life today. By its nature, it is a kind of elemental thought that attempts to establish a spiritual relationship between man and the universe. Mysticism does not believe that logical reasoning can achieve this unity, and it therefore retreats into intuition, where imagination has free rein. In a certain sense, then, mysticism goes back to a mode of thinking that takes roundabout routes.

Since we only accept knowledge that is based on truth attained through logical reasoning, the convictions on which mysticism is founded cannot become our own. Moreover, they are not satisfying in themselves. Of all the mysticism of the past it must be said that its ethical content is slight. It puts men on the road of inwardness, but not on that of a viable ethic. The truth of philosophy is not proved until it has led us to experience the relationship between our being and that of the universe, an experience that makes us genuine human beings, guided by an active ethic.

Against the spiritual void of our age, neither nonelemental thought with its long-winded interpretations of the world nor the intuition of mysticism can do anything effective.

The great German philosophical systems of the early nineteenth century were greeted with enthusiasm, yet they prepared the ground on which skepticism developed.

In order to become thinking beings again, people must rediscover their ability to think, so they can attain the knowledge and wisdom they need to truly live. The thinking that starts from Reverence for Life is a renewal of elemental thinking. The stream that has been flowing for a long distance underground resurfaces again.

The belief that elemental thought can lead us today to an affirmative ethic of life and the world, for which it has searched in the past in vain, is no illusion.

The world does not consist of phenomena only; it is also alive. I must establish a relationship with my life in this world, insofar as it is within my reach, one that is not only passive but active. In dedicating myself to the service of whatever lives, I find an activity that has meaning and purpose.

The idea of Reverence for Life offers itself as the realistic answer to the realistic question of how man and the universe are related to each other. Of the universe, man knows only that everything that exists is, like himself, a manifestation of the will to live. With this universe, he stands in both a passive and an active relationship. On the one hand he is subject to the flow of world events; on the other hand he is able to preserve and build, or to injure and destroy, the life that surrounds him.

The only possible way of giving meaning to his existence is to raise his physical relationship to the world to a spiritual one. If he remains a passive being, through resignation he enters into a spiritual relationship with the world. True resignation consists in this: that man, feeling his subordination to the course of world events, makes his way toward inward freedom from the fate that shapes his external existence. Inward freedom gives him the strength to triumph over the difficulties of everyday life and to become a deeper and more inward person, calm and peaceful. Resignation, therefore, is the spiritual and ethical affirmation of one's own existence. Only he who has gone through the trial of resignation is capable of accepting the world.

By playing an active role, man enters into a spiritual relationship with this world that is quite different: he does not see his existence in isolation. On the contrary, he is united with the lives that surround him; he experiences the destinies of others as his own. He helps as much as he can and realizes that there is no greater happiness than to participate in the development and protection of life.

Once man begins to think about the mystery of his life and the links connecting him with the life that fills the world, he cannot but accept, for his own life and all other life that surrounds him, the principle of Reverence for Life. He will act according to this principle of the ethical affirmation of life in everything he does. His life will become in every respect more difficult than if he lived for himself, but at the same time it will be richer, more beautiful, and happier. It will become, instead of mere living, a genuine experience of life.

Beginning to think about life and the world leads us directly and almost irresistibly to Reverence for Life. No other conclusions make any sense.

If the man who has begun to think wishes to persist in merely vegetating, he can do so only by submitting to a life devoid of thought. If he perseveres in his thinking he will arrive at Reverence for Life.

Any thought that claims to lead to skepticism or life without ethical ideals is not genuine thought but thoughtlessness disguised as thinking. This is manifested by the absence of any interest in the mystery of life and the world.

Reverence for Life in itself contains resignation, an affirmative attitude toward the world, and ethics. These are the three essential and inseparable elements of a worldview that is the result (or fruit) of thinking.

Because it has its origin in realistic thinking, the ethic of Reverence for Life is realistic, and leads man to a realistic and clear confrontation with reality.

It may look, at first glance, as if Reverence for Life were something too general and too lifeless to provide the content for a living ethic. But thinking need not worry about whether its expressions sound lively, so long as they hit the mark and have life in them. Anyone who comes under the influence of the ethic of Reverence for Life will very soon be able to detect, thanks to what that ethic demands from him, the fire that glows in the seemingly abstract expression. The ethic of Reverence for Life is the ethic of love widened into universality. It is the ethic of Jesus, now recognized as a logical consequence of thought.

Some object that this ethic sets too high a value on natural life. To this one can respond that the mistake made by all previous ethical systems has been the failure to recognize that life as such is the mysterious value with which they have to deal. Reverence for Life, therefore, is applied to natural life and the life of the mind alike. In the parable of Jesus, the shepherd saves not merely the soul of the lost sheep but the whole animal. The stronger the reverence for natural life, the stronger also that for spiritual life.

The ethic of Reverence for Life is judged particularly strange because it establishes no dividing line between higher and lower, between more valuable and less valuable life. It has its reasons for this omission.

To undertake to establish universally valid distinctions of value between different kinds of life will end in judging them by the greater or lesser distance at which they stand from us human beings. Our own judgment is, however, a purely subjective criterion. Who among us knows what significance any other kind of life has in itself, as a part of the universe?

From this distinction comes the view that there can be life that is worthless, which can be willfully destroyed. Then in the category of worthless life we may classify various kinds of insects, or primitive peoples, according to circumstances.

To the person who is truly ethical all life is sacred, including that which from the human point of view seems lower. Man makes distinctions only as each case comes before him, and under the pressure of necessity, as, for example, when it falls to him to decide which of two lives he must sacrifice in order to preserve the other. But all through this series of decisions he is conscious of acting on subjective grounds and arbitrarily, and knows that he bears the responsibility for the life that is sacrificed.

I rejoice over the new remedies for sleeping sickness, which enable me to preserve life, where once I could only witness the progress of a painful disease. But every time I put the germs that cause the disease under the microscope I cannot but reflect that I have to sacrifice this life in order to save another.

I bought from some villagers a young osprey they had caught on a sandbank, in order to rescue it from their cruel hands. But then I had to decide whether I should let it starve, or kill a number of small fishes every day in order to keep it alive. I decided on the latter course, but every day the responsibility to sacrifice one life for another caused me pain.

Standing, as all living beings are, before this dilemma of the will to live, man is constantly forced to preserve his own life and life in general only at the cost of other life. If he has been touched by the ethic of Reverence for Life, he injures and destroys life only under a necessity he cannot avoid, and never from thoughtlessness.

Devoted as I was from boyhood to the cause of protecting animal life, it is a special joy to me that the universal ethic of Reverence for Life shows such sympathy with animals— so often represented as sentimentality—to be an obligation no thinking person can escape. Past ethics faced the problem of the relationship between man and animal either without sensitivity or as being incomprehensible. Even when there was sympathy with animal creation, it could not be brought within the scope of ethics because ethics focused solely on the behavior of man to man.

Will the time ever come when public opinion will no longer tolerate popular amusements that depend on the maltreatment of animals!

The ethic, then, that originates in thinking is not "rational," but irrational and enthusiastic. It does not draw a circle of well-defined tasks around me, but charges each individual with responsibility for all life within his reach and forces him to devote himself to helping that life.

Any profound view of the universe is mystic in that it brings men into a spiritual relationship with the Infinite. The concept of Reverence for Life is ethical mysticism. It allows union with the Infinite to be realized by ethical action. This ethical mysticism originates in logical thinking. If our will to live begins to meditate about itself and the universe, we will become sensitive to life around us and will then, insofar as it is possible, dedicate through our actions our own will to live to that of the infinite will to live. Rational thinking, if it goes deep, ends of necessity in the irrational realm of mysticism. It has, of course, to deal with life and the world, both of which are nonrational entities.

In the universe the infinite will to live reveals itself to us as will to create, and this is filled with dark and painful riddles for us. It manifests itself in us as the will to love, which resolves the riddles through our actions. The concept of Reverence for Life therefore has a religious character.

The person who adopts and acts upon this belief is motivated by a piety that is elemental.

With its active ethic of love, and through its spirituality, the concept of the world that is based on respect for life is in essence related to Christianity and to all religions that profess the ethic of love. Now we can establish a lively relationship between Christianity and thought that we never before had in our spiritual life.

In the eighteenth century Christianity in the time of rationalism entered into an alliance with thought. It was able to do so because at that time it encountered an enthusiastic ethic that was religious in character. Thought itself had not produced this ethic, however, but had unwittingly taken it over from Christianity. When, later on, it had to depend solely upon its own ethic, this proved to have so little life and so little religion that it had not much in common with Christian ethics. As a consequence, the bonds between Christianity and active thought were loosened. Today Christianity has withdrawn into itself and is occupied with the propagation of its own ideas. It no longer considers it important to keep ideas in agreement with thought, but prefers to regard them as something altogether outside of, and superior to, rational thought. Christianity thereby loses its connection with the elemental spirit of the times and the possibility of exercising any real influence over it.

The philosophy of Reverence for Life once again poses the question of whether Christianity will or will not join hands with a form of thought that is both ethical and religious in character.

To become aware of its real self, Christianity needs thought. For centuries it treasured the great commandments of love and mercy as traditional truths without opposing slavery, witch burning, torture, and all the other ancient and medieval forms of inhumanity committed in its name. Only when it experienced the influence of the thinking of the Enlightenment was Christianity stirred up to enter the struggle for humanitarian principles. This remembrance ought to keep it forever from assuming any air of arrogance vis-à-vis thought.

Many people find pleasure today in recalling how "superficial" Christianity became in the Enlightenment. It is, however, only fair to acknowledge to what degree this "superficial" character was balanced by the services Christianity rendered in this period.

Today torture has been reestablished. In many countries the system of justice quietly tolerates torture being applied before and simultaneously with the regular proceedings of police and prison officials in order to extract confessions from those accused. The amount of suffering thus caused every hour surpasses imagination. To this renewal of torture Christianity today offers no opposition even in words, much less in deeds.

Because Christianity hardly acts on its spiritual or ethical principles, it deceives itself with the delusion that its position as a Church becomes stronger every year. It is accommodating itself to the spirit of the age by adopting a kind of modern worldliness. Like other organized bodies it tries to prove itself by becoming an ever stronger and more uniform organization, justified and recognized through its role in history and its institutions. But as it gains in external power, it loses in spiritual power.

Christianity cannot take the place of thinking, but it must be founded on it. In and by itself it is not capable of overcoming thoughtlessness and skepticism. Only an age that draws its strength from thought and from an elemental piety can recognize the imperishable character of Christianity.

Just as a stream is kept from gradually drying up because it flows along above underground water, so Christianity needs the underground water of elemental piety that issues from thinking. It can only attain real spiritual power when men no longer find the road from thought to religion barred.

I know that I myself owe it to thought that I was able to retain my faith in religion.

The thinking person stands up more freely in the face of traditional religious truth than the nonthinking person and feels the intrinsic, profound, and imperishable elements much more strongly.

Anyone who has recognized that the idea of love is the spiritual ray of light that reaches us from the infinite ceases to demand from religion that it offer him complete knowledge of the metaphysical. He ponders, indeed, the great questions: What is the meaning of evil in the world? How in God, the source of being, are the will to create and the will to love one? In what relation do the spiritual life and the material life stand to one another? And in what way is our existence transitory and yet eternal? But he is able to leave these questions unanswered, however painful that may be. In the knowledge of his spiritual union with God through love he possesses all that is necessary.

"Love never faileth: but whether there be knowledge it shall be done away," says Paul.

The deeper is piety, the humbler are its claims with regard to knowledge of the metaphysical. It is like a path that winds between the hills instead of running over them.

The fear that a Christianity that sees the origin of piety in thought will sink into pantheism is without foundation. All living Christianity is pantheistic, since it regards everything that exists as having its origin in the source of all being. But at the same time all ethical piety is superior to any pantheistic mysticism, in that it does not find the God of love in nature, but knows about Him only from the fact that He announces Himself in us as the will to love. The First Cause of Being, as He manifests Himself in nature, is to us always impersonal. To the First Cause of Being that is revealed to us in the will to love, however, we relate as to an ethical personality.

The belief that the Christianity that has been influenced by rational thought has lost its ability to appeal to man's conscience, to his sinfulness, is unfounded. We cannot see that sin has diminished where it has been much talked about. There is not much about it in the Sermon on the Mount. But thanks to the longing for deliverance from sin and for purity of heart that Jesus has included in the Beatitudes, these form the great call to repentance that is unceasingly working on man.

If Christianity, for the sake of any tradition or for any considerations whatever, refuses to let itself be interpreted in terms of ethical religious thinking, it will be a misfortune for itself and for mankind. Christianity needs to be filled with the spirit of Jesus, and in the strength of that shall spiritualize itself into the living religion of inwardness and love that is its destiny. Only then can it become the leaven in the spiritual life of mankind.

What has been presented as Christianity during these nineteen centuries is merely a beginning, full of mistakes, not a full-grown Christianity springing from the spirit of Jesus.

Because I am deeply devoted to Christianity, I am trying to serve it with loyalty and sincerity. I do not attempt to defend it with the fragile and ambiguous arguments of Christian apologetics. I demand from Christianity that it reform itself in the spirit of sincerity and with thoughtfulness, so it may become conscious of its true nature.

To the question of whether I am a pessimist or an optimist, I answer that my knowledge is pessimistic, but my willing and hoping are optimistic.

I am pessimistic because I feel the full weight of what we conceive to be the absence of purpose in the course of world events. Only at rare moments have I felt really glad to be alive. I cannot help but feel the suffering all around me, not only of humanity but of the whole of creation.

I have never tried to withdraw myself from this community of suffering. It seemed to me a matter of course that we should all take our share of the burden of pain that lies upon the world. Even while I was a boy at school it was clear to me that no explanation of the evil in the world could ever satisfy me; all explanations, I felt, ended in sophistries, and at bottom had no other object than to minimize our sensitivity to the misery around us. That a thinker like Leibnitz could reach the miserable conclusion that though this world is, indeed, not good, it is the best that is possible, I have never been able to understand.

But however concerned I was with the suffering in the world, I never let myself become lost in brooding over it. I always held firmly to the thought that each one of us can do a little to bring some portion of it to an end. Thus I gradually came to the conclusion that all we can understand about the problem is that we must follow our own way as those who want to bring about deliverance.

I am also pessimistic about the current world situation. I cannot persuade myself that it is better than it appears to be. I feel that we are on a fatal road, that if we continue to follow it, it will bring us into a new "Dark Ages." I see before me, in all its dimensions, the spiritual and material misery to which mankind has surrendered because it has renounced thinking and the ideals that thought engenders.

And yet I remain optimistic. One belief from my childhood I have preserved with a certainty I can never lose: belief in truth. I am confident that the spirit generated by truth is stronger than the force of circumstances. In my view no other destiny awaits mankind than that which, through its mental and spiritual disposition, it prepares for itself. Therefore I do not believe that it will have to tread the road to ruin right to the end.

If people can be found who revolt against the spirit of thoughtlessness and are sincere and profound enough to spread the ideals of ethical progress, we will witness the emergence of a new spiritual force strong enough to evoke a new spirit in mankind.

Because I have confidence in the power of truth and of the spirit, I believe in the future of mankind. Ethical acceptance of the world contains within itself an optimistic willing and hoping that can never be lost. It is, therefore, never afraid to face the somber reality as it really is.

In my own life, I had times in which anxiety, trouble, and sorrow were so overwhelming that, had my nerves not been so strong, I might have broken down under the weight. Heavy is the burden of fatigue and responsibility that has lain upon me without a break for years. I have not had much of my life for myself. But I have had blessings too: that I am allowed to work in the service of compassion; that my work has been successful; that I receive from other people affection and kindness in abundance; that I have loyal helpers who consider my work as their own; that I enjoy a health that allows me to undertake the most exhausting work; that I have a well-balanced temperament, which varies little, and an energy that can be exerted with calm and deliberation; and that I can recognize whatever happiness I feel and accept it as a gift.

I am also deeply grateful that I can work in freedom at a time when an oppressive dependence is the fate of so many. Though my immediate work is practical, I also have opportunities to pursue my spiritual and intellectual interests.

That the circumstances of my life have provided such favorable conditions for my work, I accept as a blessing for which I hope to prove worthy.

How much of the work I have planned shall I be able to complete?

My hair is beginning to turn gray. My body is beginning to show signs of the exertions I have demanded of it and of the passage of the years.

I look back with gratitude to the time when, without having to husband my strength, I could pursue my physical and mental activities without interruption.

I look forward to the future with calmness and humility so that I may be prepared for renunciation if it be required of me. Whether we are active or suffering, we must find the courage of those who have struggled to achieve the peace that passeth all understanding.

Lambaréné
MARCH 7, 1931

Chronology

1875	January 14, born in Kaysersberg, Alsace. During the year, family moved to Günsbach.
1880	First music instruction.
1880–1884	Attended village school in Günsbach.
1883	First played the organ.
Autumn 1884– Autumn 1885	Attended Realschule in Münster/Alsace in preparation for the Gymnasium.
Autumn 1885– August 1893	Attended Gymnasium in Mülhausen/Alsace.
1893	October, first sojourn in Paris. Studied organ with Widor.
1893– Spring 1898	Studied theology, philosophy, and musical theory at University of Strasbourg.

April 1894– April 1895	Military service with infantry at Strasbourg.
1896	Decided to devote life to service of humanity beginning at age thirty.
1898	May 6, passed first theological examination before faculty. First publication: *Eugene Munch: 1857–1898*.
October 1898– March 1899	Second sojourn in Paris. Again studied under Widor.
1899	April–July, studied philosophy and organ in Berlin. July, received Ph.D. at Strasbourg. December, *The Religious Philosophy of Kant* published. Appointed to staff of Church of St. Nicholai's in Strasbourg.
1900	"Die Philosophie und die Allgemeine Bildung" published. July 21, obtained licentiate degree in theology, Strasbourg. September 23, ordained as a regular curate, St. Nicholai, Strasbourg.
1901	Publication of *The Mystery of the Kingdom of God*. May–September, provisional appointment at St. Thomas theological seminary in Strasbourg.
1903	October, appointed principal of the theological seminary in Strasbourg.
1904	Sees article about needs of protestant mission in Gabon. Decides to serve as missionary there himself.

1905   *J. S. Bach le musicien-poète* published in
                Paris. October 13, informed friends of de-
                cision to study medicine, serve in Africa.
                October, resigned his post at the theological
                seminary.

1905–1912   Medical studies, University of Strasbourg.

1906   *The Art of Organ-Building and Organ-Play-
                ing in Germany and France* and *The Quest
                of the Historical Jesus* published.

1908   *J. S. Bach* published.

1909   Third Congress of the International Music
                Society in Vienna. Schweitzer responsible
                for formulation of *Internationales Regulativ
                für Orgelbau.*

1911   Published *Paul and His Interpreters.* De-
                cember, passed his medical examinations.

1912   Spring, resigned his post at St. Nicholai.
                June 18, married Helene Bresslau. First two
                volumes of Bach's *Complete Organ Works*
                published with Widor.

1913   February, granted M.D. *Psychiatric Study
                of Jesus* published. Second edition of *The
                Quest of the Historical Jesus* published. Vol-
                umes 3–5 of Bach's *Complete Organ Works*
                published. March 26, departed for Lamba-
                réné with his wife. Arrived April 16.

1913–1917   First sojourn in Lambaréné.

1914	August–November, interned as enemy alien at Lambaréné.
1915	September, concept of Reverence for Life came to him during Ogowe River journey.
Autumn 1917–Summer 1918	Leaves Africa as prisoner of war, internment in Bordeaux, Garaison, and St. Rémy.
1918	July, returned to Günsbach. Illness.
1919–April 1921	Again served at St. Nicholai, and as a doctor in the Strasbourg city hospital.
1919	January 14, daughter Rhena born.
1920	In Sweden for lectures at the University of Uppsala. Also lectures and concerts to raise money for Lambaréné. Awarded honorary doctorate in divinity by the theological faculty of the University of Zürich.
1921	*On the Edge of the Primeval Forest* published.
1921–1922	Lectures and concerts in Switzerland, England, Sweden, and Denmark.
1923	*The Philosophy of Civilization* published. *Christianity and the Religions of the World* published in English; German translation in 1924.
1924	*Memoirs of Childhood and Youth* published.
April 1924–July 1927	Second sojourn in Lambaréné, this time without his wife, who remains in Europe with daughter.

1925   *More from the Primeval Forest*, Part I, published.

1926   *More from the Primeval Forest*, Part II, published.

1927   January 21, moved hospital to new site near Lambaréné.

July 1927–
December 1929   Lectures in Sweden, Denmark, Holland, Great Britain, Czechoslovakia, and Switzerland. Concerts in Germany. Presented Universal Order of Human Merit at Geneva for services to civilization and humanity. Presented honorary Ph.D. from the University of Prague.

1928   August 28, received Goethe Prize from the city of Frankfurt. *More from the Primeval Forest*, Part III, published.

December 1929–
February 1932   Third sojourn in Africa. His wife joined him until Easter 1930.

1929   *Selbstdarstellung* published. Awarded honorary doctorates in theology and philosophy, University of Edinburgh.

1930   *The Mysticism of Paul the Apostle* published.

1931   *Out of My Life and Thought* published. Awarded honorary doctorate in music, University of Edinburgh.

February 1932–
April 1933   In Europe for lectures and concerts.

1932   March 22, Goethe Gedenkrede, Frankfurt.
                        June, awarded honorary doctorate in theol-
                        ogy from Oxford and honorary LL.D. from
                        St. Andrew's. July, "Goethe als Denker und
                        Mensch," Ulm.

April 1933–   Fourth sojourn in Africa, again without his
January 1934   wife.

February 1934–   In Europe.
February 1935

1934   October, Hibbert Lectures, Manchester
                        College, Oxford: "Religion in Modern Civ-
                        ilization." November, Gifford Lectures in
                        Edinburgh, resulting in separate book on *In-
                        dian Thought and Its Development*, pub-
                        lished in same year.

1935   February–August, fifth sojourn in Lamba-
                        réné, again without his wife.

September 1935–   In Europe. Second series of Gifford Lec-
February 1937   tures. Lectures and concerts in England. Re-
                        corded Bach organ music for Columbia
                        Records.

1936   *African Hunting Stories* published in book
                        form.

February 1937–   Sixth sojourn in Lambaréné, without his
January 1939   wife.

1938   *From My African Notebook* published.

1939	February, arrived in Europe; returned immediately to Lambaréné because of danger of war.
March 1939–October 1949	Seventh sojourn in Lambaréné. His wife joined him from 1941 to 1946.
1948	*The Jungle Hospital* and *Goethe: Two Addresses* published.
October 1948–October 1949	Mostly in Europe.
1949	June 11, awarded honorary LL.D. by the University of Chicago. July, Goethe Bicentennial Convocation in Aspen, Colorado. *Goethe: Drei Reden* published.
October 1949–June 1951	Eighth sojourn in Lambaréné. His wife joined him until June 1950.
1950	*Goethe: Vier Reden* published. *A Pelican Tells About His Life* published in book form.
1951	July, returned to Europe. Made further recordings for Columbia. September 16, Peace Prize of the West German Book Publishers. December 3, elected to the French Academy.
December 1951–July 1952	Ninth sojourn in Lambaréné.
July–December 1952	In Europe for lectures and recitals. September, awarded Paracelsus Medal by the German Medical Society. October, speech before the French Academy. Received

Prince Carl Medal, grand medal of the Swedish Red Cross. Installed as a member of the Swedish Royal Academy of Music and awarded an honorary doctorate in theology by the University of Marburg.

December 1952– June 1954	Tenth sojourn in Lambaréné.
1953	October, awarded the Nobel Peace Prize for 1952. Awarded honorary degree by University of Kapstadt.
June– December 1954	In Europe. Volume 6 of Bach's *Complete Organ Works* published with Édouard Nies-Berger. April, letter to the *London Daily Herald* concerning the H-bomb. November 4, Nobel Peace Prize speech, "The Problem of Peace in the World of Today," in Oslo.
December 1954– July 1955	Eleventh sojourn in Lambaréné. January 14, 1955, eightieth birthday celebrated in Lambaréné.
July– December 1955	In Europe. Received Order of Merit in London; Orden pour le Mérite, Germany; and honorary J.D., Cambridge University.
December 1955– June 1957	Twelfth sojourn in Lambaréné. Helene with him until May 22, 1957.
1957	April 23, first nuclear test ban broadcast. June 1, Helene Schweitzer-Bresslau died in Zürich. June 21–December 4, in Europe. Visited Switzerland and Germany.
December 1957– August 1959	Thirteenth sojourn in Lambaréné.

1958   April 28, 29, 30, three addresses over Norwegian radio about nuclear war. Published as *Peace or Atomic War*. Awarded honorary M.D., University of Münster. Awarded honorary Dr. Theol., Tübingen.

1959   March 23, awarded Sonning Prize in Copenhagen for "work to the benefit of European culture." August to December, in Europe. September 29, accepted Sonning Prize in Copenhagen. November 18, awarded Joseph Lemaire Prize in Brussels. December, fourteenth and final departure for Lambaréné.

1960   January 14, eighty-fifth birthday celebrated in Lambaréné.

1963   *Die Lehre der Ehrfurcht vor dem Leben* published.

1965   January 14, ninetieth birthday celebrated in Lambaréné. September 4, died in Lambaréné.

1966   *Reverence for Life (Strassburger Predigten)* published posthumously.

Bibliography

Selected Titles by Albert Schweitzer

Note: For *all* titles the first publication date in English is listed.

Christianity and the Religions of the World. London: Allen and Unwin, 1923.

Civilization and Ethics. (Part 2 of *The Philosophy of Civilization*.) London: Black, 1923.

The Decay and the Restoration of Civilization. (Part 1 of *The Philosophy of Civilization*.) London: Black, 1923.

The Essence of Faith: Philosophy and Religion. New York: Philosophical Library, 1966.

The Forest Hospital at Lambaréné. New York: Henry Holt, 1931.

From My African Notebook. London: Allen and Unwin, 1938.

Goethe. Address delivered on receiving the Goethe Prize in Frankfurt. New York: Henry Holt, 1928.

Goethe: Five Studies. Boston: Beacon, 1961.

Indian Thought and Its Development. London: Hodder and Stoughton; New York: Henry Holt, 1936.

J. S. Bach. 2 vols. London: Black; New York: Macmillan, 1938.

The Kingdom of God and Primitive Christianity. London: Black; New York: Seaburg, 1968.

Memoirs of Childhood and Youth. London: Allen and Unwin, 1924.

The Mystery of the Kingdom of God: The Secret of Jesus' Messiahship and Passion. London: Black; New York: Dodd and Mead, 1914.

The Mysticism of Paul the Apostle. London: Black; New York: Henry Holt, 1931.

On the Edge of the Primeval Forest. London: Black, 1922.

Organ-Building and Organ-Playing in France and Germany. London: Black, 1953.

Paul and His Interpreters. London: Black; New York: Macmillan, 1912.

Peace or Atomic War? Three Appeals. London: Black; New York: Holt, Rinehart and Winston, 1958.

The Philosophy of Civilization. 2 vols. in 1. New York: Macmillan, 1949.

The Problem of Peace in the World Today. Nobel Peace Prize acceptance speech. London: Black; New York: Harper, 1954.

The Psychiatric Study of Jesus: Exposition and Criticism. Boston: Beacon, 1948.

The Quest of the Historical Jesus. London: Black, 1910.

Reverence for Life. Sermons 1900–1919. New York: Harper and Row, 1969.

The Story of My Pelican. London: Souvenir, 1964.

Anthologies of Essays and of Excerpts from Schweitzer's Writings

Cousins, Norman. *The Words of Albert Schweitzer*. New York: Newmarket, 1984.

Jack, Homer. *On Nuclear War and Peace*. Elgin, Ill.: Brethren, 1988.

Joy, Charles. *Albert Schweitzer*. Boston: Beacon, 1947.

Books About Albert Schweitzer

Anderson, Erica. *The Albert Schweitzer Album: A Portrait in Words and Pictures*. London: Black; New York: Harper and Row, 1965.

Brabazon, James. *Albert Schweitzer: A Biography*. New York: Putnam, 1975.

Cousins, Norman. *Albert Schweitzer's Mission: Healing and Peace*. New York and London: Norton, 1985.

Cousins, Norman. *Doctor Schweitzer of Lambaréné*. London: Black; New York: Harper and Row, 1960.

Joy, Charles, and Melvin Arnold. *The Africa of Albert Schweitzer*. New York: Harper, 1949.

Marshall, George, and David Poling. *Schweitzer: A Biography*. London: Bles; New York: Doubleday, 1971.

Picht, Werner. *The Life and Thought of Albert Schweitzer*. London: Allen and Unwin, 1964.

Roback, A. A., ed. *The Albert Schweitzer Jubilee Book*. Cambridge, Mass.: Sci-Art, 1945.

Seaver, George. *Albert Schweitzer: The Man and His Mind*. London: Black, 1947.

Film and Videotape

The Living Work of Albert Schweitzer. Erica Anderson and Rhena Schweitzer. 1965. 16mm film, color, 35 min.

The Spirit of Albert Schweitzer. John Scudder. Video, color, 33 min. VHS, Beta or ¾″ format.

Other

Bach's Complete Organ Works. Edited by Albert Schweitzer, Charles-Marie Widor, and Edouard Niels-Berger. Vols. 1–8. New York: Schirmer, 1902–1964.

Griffith, Nancy Snell, and Laura Person. *Albert Schweitzer: An International Bibliography*. Boston: G. K. Hall, 1981.

For further information about Albert Schweitzer, readers are welcome to contact the Albert Schweitzer Center, Hurlburt Road, R.D. 1, Box 7, Great Barrington, MA 01230 (413-528-3124).

Index